THE IMAGINED CITY

THE IMAGINED CITY
A LITERARY HISTORY OF WINNIPEG

EDITED BY

DAVID ARNASON & MHARI MACKINTOSH

TURNSTONE PRESS

Turnstone Press
Artspace Building
607-100 Arthur Street
Winnipeg, MB
R3B 1H3 Canada
www.TurnstonePress.com

Turnstone Press gratefully acknowledges the assistance of The Canada Council for the Arts, the Manitoba Arts Council, the Government of Canada through the Book Publishing Industry Development Program and the Government of Manitoba through the Department of Culture, Heritage and Tourism, Arts Branch, for our publishing activities.

Cover design: Doowah Design
Interior design: Sharon Caseburg
Maps: Weldon Hiebert
Printed and bound in Canada by Friesens for Turnstone Press.

Library and Archives Canada Cataloguing in Publication

   The imagined city : a literary history of Winnipeg / edited by David Arnason and Mhari Mackintosh.

Includes bibliographical references and index.
ISBN 0-88801-298-5

   1. Winnipeg (Man.)—Literary collections. 2. Winnipeg (Man.)—In literature. 3. Winnipeg (Man.)—Intellectual life. 4. Canadian literature (English). I. Arnason, David, 1940- II. Mackintosh, Mhari, 1948- III. Title.

PS8237.W55I43 2005   C810.8'032712743   C2005-906498-6

About the front cover:

Main Street north of Portage, Winnipeg, c. 1897. Archives of Manitoba, Thomas Burns Collection, 568-1.

About the back cover:

Police as "Teddy Bears," University of Manitoba Archives and Special Collections, Winnipeg Tribune Collection, 18-6254-197.

Queen Victoria dressed in snow, copyright © Dennis Fast.

Rose Amy Fyleman (1877–1957) was born on March 6, 1877, in Basford, Nottinghamshire, England. She wrote dozens of poems about fairies, but is most remembered for the lines, "There are fairies at the bottom of our garden," and "I think mice are rather nice." Few Manitoba children can have escaped learning her poem about Queen Victoria.

CONTENTS

ACKNOWLEDGEMENTS

Many people were very helpful in putting together this collection. We would like to thank Sharon Foley, Photo Archivist at the Provincial Archives, and also Bronwen Quarry at the Provincial Archives. The staff at Archives & Special Collections at the University of Manitoba was especially helpful. Shelley Sweeney, the chief archivist, allowed us to invade her premises and introduced us to her staff. Lewis St. George Stubbs knows more about images of Winnipeg than anyone alive, and he is a walking encyclopaedia of Winnipeg information. Michelle Strutt, Office Assistant at the university archives, located pictures we thought we would never find. Hugh Larimer, Maps Librarian at the Dafoe Library at the University of Manitoba, helped us to locate maps, and when we needed to make the maps ourselves, Weldon Hiebert from the University of Winnipeg made them for us. David Carr, director of the University of Manitoba Press, made helpful suggestions. Tyler Wolosewich from the Hockey Hall of Fame found us some wonderful images, and Jack Templeman, Curator, Winnipeg Police Museum, found us images we couldn't find anywhere else. Pat Sanders was our very thorough copy editor and we are grateful for her attention to detail. Ben McPhee-Sigurdson searched for photos in many archives.

Finally, we would like to thank the wonderful staff at Turnstone Press. Todd Besant spent many long hours finding permissions. Kelly Stifora offered helpful advice, and our special thanks go to our editor, Sharon Caseburg, who practically put her life on hold to get the book out.

David Arnason & Mhari Mackintosh

INTRODUCTION

All great cities are known more by their representations in art than by their economic or military greatness. London is forever foggy however the British clean it up, because Dickens made it foggy, and dozens of other writers, painters, and filmmakers followed suit. Rio basks in eternal sunlight. New York is brash and self-assured and hectic. But what of Winnipeg? Is it the steamy ethnic North End given us by such writers as Adele Wiseman and John Marlyn, or is it the Red River settlement where the Métis fiddle and jig and dance with the Governor recently sent from Scotland or England? Is it the booming raw new city with brothels and bars on every corner, or is it a vast collection of suburbs where ad executives return for their evening martini before collapsing in front of the television set? Winnipeg became a city in 1874, but there was a proto-city before that, a collection of people who began to give Winnipeg a character and a shape. It took a couple of thousand years to make Rome, but Winnipeg has moved from a settlement to a sophisticated second-millennium city in a remarkably short time.

Of course Winnipeg is all these cities, city upon city laid over the palimpsest of earlier cities, a kind of living archive of the mix of cultures that made this place. About seventy percent of Manitoba's population lives in a single city, Winnipeg, and this has been the case for most of the past century. Manitoba is one of the most urban areas anywhere, and though there has been a steady and continuing move from the country to the city, most Manitobans are profoundly urban, and have been that way for several generations. The image of the urban child driving out to visit Grandpa and Grandma on the farm is a cliché that has already passed. Grandpa and Grandma are much more likely to live in a high-rise.

The earliest cities arose as places for storing grain and building temples. The complex organization of large population centres did much to create what we think of as civilization. The dynamics of city organization encouraged the emergence of specialists and professionals. You need a large population to support such specialists as carpenters and masons and architects and engineers. In a rural setting each person must be his own carpenter, mason, or architect.

Large populations create what we think of as culture and entertainment. You need leisure to attend cultural or sporting events. You need surplus capital to pay people to engage in the production of theatre and music and spectacle. You need armies to defend your cities, and you need a vast array of services to support your armies. Early cities were walled cities, and it is still profitable to think of cities as having an inside and an outside. Winnipeg is a great multicultural city because it has enfolded into itself the cultures of the world.

What we think of as civilization is very largely the product of the rise of cities. The great cultural cities of the world are rooted back in a nearly undiscoverable history. They were always already there. But Winnipeg, like most New World cities, has a definable and knowable history. It is a speeded-up example of how a city can rise, and, in Winnipeg's case, in some respects, decline. We like to think of Winnipeg as a subject, a personality, and a kind of psychiatric case study. We can speak of Winnipeg as friendly or unfriendly, proud, brash, retiring, self-deprecating or egotistical. We can apply most of the words that define the qualities of human beings to cities. We know, for instance, that Toronto is a bit insular and arrogant, unsure of itself but swaggering nevertheless. Vancouver is laid back, a trifle decadent. Montreal is sophisticated and European. Calgary talks too loud and is unstable. Ottawa is greying and dull. Saskatoon is nice, but a bit of a hayseed. Of course, none of these descriptions has an ounce of value to it, and each would be hotly disputed by the inhabitants of those places. But this is a Winnipeg-centric book and we can say what we like.

We began by thinking of Winnipeg as an unformed city, Winnipeg as the confluence of the Assiniboine and the Red and the events that took place there. At some historically unavailable period, it was pure nature, the meeting of two rivers, a site for birds and animals and insects. Then it became a stopping place for Aboriginal people, and later the site where the Selkirk settlers and the Métis merged in the evolution of a new sort of society. There was no inside and outside then. No Winnipeg. Winnipeg didn't come into existence until January 1, 1874, and in that earlier period the Winnipeg we know was not anticipated. The fur traders of the Hudson's Bay Company and the North West Company moved across the landscape and through the settlement. Whether it was called Fort Garry or the Selkirk Settlement or the Red River Settlement, it was less a defined place than a destination or a stopping place or a crossroads. It had not yet begun to define or represent itself.

Then, on December 13, 1873, the Winnipeg Act was passed and on January 4, 1874, Winnipeg came into existence. The city came to consciousness. The incorporation of Winnipeg was an act of arrogance. The new city had 3700 people, not much competition for Paris, London, or New York, but a city, nevertheless, complete with a charter. And immediately, the city began to represent itself to itself, to try to define what it was. And whatever it was, it was not modest. It declared itself the Chicago of the North. It saw itself as a site of endless possibility, and the great boom of the early 1880s gave it every reason for confidence.

Winnipeg was on the move. Its population increased to 14,700 by 1882. It had a bar for every 200 people. It had a large number of variety theatres. It had sufficient brothels to console the huge supply of single males who had come to make their fortunes, and it had a myriad of churches and educational institutes for those who chose more conservative consolation.

Winnipeg began to see itself as a great city, and a great city needs great architecture. In the period from 1880 to 1900 the city constructed some of the wonderful buildings that still make it a centre for the film industry when it wants to represent turn-of-the-century America. Winnipeg borrowed its architecture from New York and Chicago and Philadelphia. Now, in a delicious irony, if New York and Chicago and Philadelphia want to represent their own pasts, they have to turn to Winnipeg.

Unfortunately, we have lost some of the grand monuments. The wonderful pink confection that was the old city hall, built in 1886 and demolished in 1964, is only a memory. We still have some of the old luxurious mansions brought by the sudden wealth of the boom, such as Mark Cameron's house on the Crescent and the Ken Howson house over on Ruskin Row. And we have the magnificence of the old Ashdown Warehouse, now newly turned into condominiums, and some of the great banks that flourished in that period.

Winnipeg also began to develop a legitimate theatre. The Walker Theatre proudly proclaimed itself one of the two or three best theatres in all North America, and it backed up that claim in 1909 when it presented *Ben Hur* on stage, complete with a race between three horse-drawn chariots running on conveyor belts and a cyclorama of the faces of Roman spectators spinning in the opposite direction to give the sense of even greater speed. It was thought at the time that special effects could go no further, though recently the films of Guy Maddin have proved them wrong. And Winnipeg became an important stop on the vaudeville circuit of North America. The great acts stopped here. Charlie Chaplin played the Walker, as did Groucho Marx. Winnipeg was to be a great international city. It would fold into itself the great art and entertainment of the world.

There are a multitude of Winnipegs. Probably the best known is the North End. It has been celebrated in such works as Adele Wiseman's *The Sacrifice,* John Marlyn's *Under the Ribs of Death,* and Ed Kleiman's *The Immortals.* It has a rich history, and the representations that exist by no means exhaust its possibilities. But there are many other Winnipegs. There is Winnipeg, the roaring boom city of the 1880s; Winnipeg, the commercial giant of the first decades of the twentieth century. There is a modernist Winnipeg, filled with flappers and pre-Depression exuberance, the French city of St. Boniface, the working-class railway cities of Weston and Transcona. There is East Kildonan, Crescentwood, and the ever-evolving West End. Each of these can be unearthed through an archaeology of the imagination.

And Winnipeg is a city haunted by ghosts. The main ghost is that of Louis Riel, who haunts the entire country, but there are plenty of other ghosts, as well. There is the ghost of Bloody Jack Kravchenko, for example, the social bandit from Winnipeg's North End who is our own version of Robin Hood, stealing from the rich and giving to the poor. Ghosts inhabit the gargoyles and cornices and signs that decorate the buildings of Main Street and Portage Avenue and the Exchange District. Every street name in Winnipeg is the trace of a ghost, either the ghost of some early settler, some other country, or some distant tragedy, as in Valour Road, named for the winners of the Victoria Gross, or Borebank Street, named for a real estate developer who went down on the *Titanic*. This gives us an advantage over other, more rational, western centres like Calgary or Regina, who numbered their streets and so removed all the nesting sites for ghosts. Actually, Winnipeg experimented with numbered streets for two years, from 1891 to 1893, but in the end, the ghosts won and we went back to names.

We have tried to choose selections from the literature about Winnipeg that will reflect its diversity. An enormous amount has been written about Winnipeg, and it would be impossible to collect all of it. We hope the selections we have chosen will give a fair picture of Winnipeg and its history. Of course, some aspects of the city have been dealt with much more thoroughly than others. The mythical North End could easily have its own book of selections from writers who have loved it or hated it, but felt compelled to represent it. So this book is about Winnipeg and not about writers. We have left out the work of many fine writers, not because what they had to say was not worthwhile, but because we were facing a feast of good literature, and often many writers had said very much the same thing. And literary quality was not our only criterion. Sometimes a clumsy statement can say more than an elegant poem.

The idea for this book came out of a course we did at the University of Manitoba. The students in that course discovered a wonderful array of writing about the city and we are grateful to them for their enthusiasm and their discoveries. They looked at Winnipeg with a fresh eye, and saw what a fascinating place they inhabited.

The buildings, the streets, the records of the city, the poems, novels and plays, these constitute our local heritage. Winnipeg is not a simple essence. It is one of the most cosmopolitan centres in the world. It has folded the outside world into the inside that is Winnipeg. We see this in our immigrant stories, but we also see it in our festivals, which are another way we represent ourselves to ourselves. The chief of these festivals is Folkorama, which celebrates our multiculturalism, and folds into Winnipeg the many countries that bring their heritages to us. It does not matter to us whether the representation of these other places is authentic or accurate. It is our Poland, our Britain, our Philippines we celebrate.

This book is a celebration of Winnipeg, one of the great but maddening cities of the world. When John Samson can write a love song to the city with the refrain "I hate Winnipeg," we have arrived at a level of sophistication that few cities can dare.

David Arnason and Mhari Mackintosh

Lt. Harry Colebourn and Winnie, mascot of the 2nd Canadian Infantry Brigade. University of Manitoba Archives and Special Collections.

THE IMAGINED CITY

EARLY RED RIVER

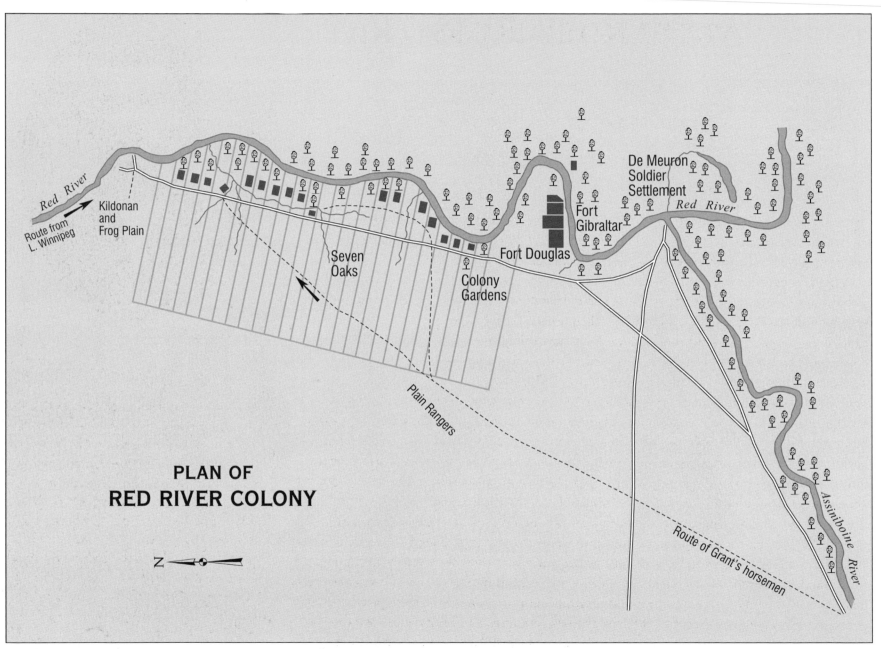

Red River

Route from
L. Winnipeg

Kildonan
and
Frog Plain

Seven
Oaks

Plain Rangers

Colony
Gardens

Fort Douglas

Fort
Gibraltar

De Meuron
Soldier
Settlement

Red River

Route of Grant's horsemen

Assiniboine River

PLAN OF
RED RIVER COLONY

N

Above: Plan of the Red River Colony. Previous page: Winnipeg 1870. Sketch from *The Romantic Settlement of Lord Selkirk's Colonists* (1909).

ALEXANDER ROSS

In Red River, as in Canada, and most other new countries, the people, for a long time, contented themselves with what are called wooden houses, of such humble appearance as might be expected where means are low, workmen scarce, and wages at a high rate. The cost of such houses depends on a variety of circumstances; but the average may be taken at 60£ sterling. These frame buildings, simple, yet commodious and comfortable, differ in size as in cost, but are seldom more than thirty feet in length, or less than twenty; the other dimensions being of corresponding proportion. A superior class of dwellings have shingled roofs, stone foundations, windows, doors and partitions panelled and painted, and the walls rough-cast with lime. One of this description, forty or fifty feet long, and well finished, will cost 300£. Such was the cost of one built for the writer; but it was the best in the settlement of its size. Of late, a decided improvement in the character of our wooden buildings has become manifest. Several are of two stories high, some with galleries, and two ornamented with verandas. Taste, as well as convenience, begins to receive its due share of consideration—the luxury of glass windows, and a lock on the outer door, things hitherto scarcely known in Red River, have become fashionable, indeed, almost general. Such houses, white as snow, look well, and have a very gay appearance.

The more solid structures of stone and lime are also, in some instances, beginning to be introduced by the Company; and this, at no distant time, will be resorted to generally, as wood is becoming scarce, even for fuel. In the upper part of the settlement, where wood may still be got, stone is not to be found; but in other places, towards the lower end, limestone quarries are abundant. Lime was made here as early as the time of Governor Bulger; but the article was only used for practical purposes, such as building and the white-washing of houses, very lately. The first instance was the building of a small powder-magazine, erected by the Company at Upper Fort Garry, in 1830. This magazine claims the proud distinction of being the first stone and lime building in the colony.

ALEXANDER ROSS (1783–1856) was a Canadian fur trader and pioneer. He was born in Scotland and came to Canada in 1805. He taught school in Upper Canada for five years, then in 1820 left for Oregon as a clerk in the Pacific Fur Company. He later worked for the North West Company and, after the amalgamation, for the Hudson's Bay Company. He wrote *Adventures of First Settlers on the Oregon or Columbia River* (1849) and *The Red River Settlement: Its Rise, Progress, and Present State* (1856).

From *The Red River Settlement: Its Rise, Progress, and Present State* by Alexander Ross (1856).

ALEXANDER BEGG

ALEXANDER BEGG was born on July 19, 1839, at Quebec. He was educated at Aberdeen and at St. John's P.Q. He came to Red River as a trader and became a business partner with Mr. A.G.B. Bannatyne. Begg wrote a number of accounts of the northwest that are still used by scholars today. His satirical novel, *Dot it Down* (1871), is the first novel written in Manitoba. The novel was meant to lampoon Charles Mair, a writer from Ontario whose articles about Red River, published in eastern Canadian newspapers, had offended Begg. He died on September 6, 1897.

D uring the winter in Red River, gaiety is the order of the day. There is so little going on in the way of business, that the settlers, to pass the time, enjoy themselves to the best of their ability. Dancing parties are of nightly occurrence, and all the weddings take place during the winter months. Indeed, a marriage is generally delayed until a large hop can be given at the same time. Weddings in Red River are no trifling affairs. We have known them to be kept up for three successive days and nights. The dances peculiar to Red River, are so spirited as a general thing, that they make the parties, as a usual thing, very pleasant and agreeable.

A few nights after the visit of Cool to "Dot," the latter received an invitation for himself and friend, to a dance, to be given in the house of one of the most respectable settlers. "Dot" took the liberty of accepting, not only for himself, but also for his friend whom we met with him at the theatre. "Dot" promised himself a great deal of fun at this party . . .

Continued

"I wish you would show me the way." This was a puzzler, and both the discomfited men were giving up in despair, when they heard the sound of sleigh bells rapidly approaching them.

"Hist!" said "Dot."

"Do you think they will run into us?" whispered his friend.

"Keep quiet," said "Dot," "they'll hear you."

"I wish they would," was the reply.

"I mean," returned "Dot," "I want to hear them."

"I'll make them hear us," said his friend, and with that he shouted out at the top of his voice.

Nearer and nearer came the approaching sleigh; and at last when it was about passing them, "Dot" roared out, "Help! For God's sake."

The stranger, who turned out to be none other than Cool, pulled up and replied, "Who are you? And where are you?"

"Stranger in a strange land," shouted "Dot." "We're in a quandary."

"You're more likely to be in a ditch."

"You're right this time," cried "Dot's" friend, "but can't you help us out? We're going to a dance, and a pretty dance we've had of it already."

Cool now alighted, and, coming up to our unfortunate party-goers, he recognized "Dot" at once.

"Hilloa, here's where you are."

"Yes!" said "Dot," "we've been here some time."

"Very unlucky," said Cool, "but we'll soon put you all right. There," he continued, after arranging matters for them, "follow me, I know the road, and we have not far to go."

Thanks to Cool's guidance, our two friends at last found themselves at the party, where they both soon forgot their adventure in the hilarity of the evening.

In one apartment, in front of a large, open log fire, sat a number of gentlemen, old fogies chiefly, talking over the events of the day. This was the refreshment and smoking room, and to it Cool conducted "Dot" and his friend. A glass of what was thought to be wine was poured out for "Dot," which he immediately swallowed at one mouthful; but alas, it turned out to be raw brandy, and the unfortunate man sputtered and gasped in an agony of torture. The old fogies started to their feet, thinking the man had taken a fit, until it was explained that he had taken brandy, supposing it to be wine. The tears streamed down "Dot's" cheeks. "Do—do—do you call—call that wine?" he managed to say. "If so it's—it's—dev—d——h strong."

Cool laughed heartily; but it was no joke for poor "Dot," and, as it turned out afterwards, was the means of getting him into serious trouble; the fact of the matter being, that the liquor went to his head.

The host now presented himself, and led the way into the dancing room, when "Dot," who had partly recovered from his unfortunate mistake, began to ingratiate himself with the ladies. It was noticed, however, that his manner became very strange, and at last it became quite plain that he was slightly elevated.

Now there is a dance in the North-West, peculiar to the country, called the Red River jig, which is as follows: A gentleman leads a lady to the middle of the floor, and at the sound of the fiddle the pair begin to dance to each other, in a regular break-down manner. This lasts until either the gentleman or the lady is relieved by one of their own sex. The second couple continue until they also give place for others, and so on this almost endless dance continues until the fiddler gives in.

"Dot," ever ready to undertake anything that offered, managed to get a partner for this description of the dance, and the gentlemen, for mischief, determined to allow him full scope for his legs. The fiddler, entering into the spirit of the joke, played his liveliest tunes. When his lady partner became tired, her place was taken by another, and so on; still no gentleman offered to relieve "Dot." The unfortunate man danced away in utter desperation, while the perspiration streamed down his face, until at last his legs began to bend under him; but to his credit, be it said, he did not give in, although towards the end of the jig he could hardly shuffle along the floor. Finally the fiddler, out of pity for the poor fellow, stopped, and "Dot" sank back exhausted to a seat. He was however, highly complimented for his pluck, and the fair ones began to form a very favourable opinion of him; but, as we will presently see, his laurels were of short duration, as he got himself into serious trouble and disgrace before the end of the party.

It happened, unfortunate for "Dot," that he held a very high opinion of himself, especially so far as it concerned his literary powers; and he was not at all backward in fishing for compliments. Finding himself, therefore, something in the light of a hero, after his jig, he took advantage of the impression he had made, by showing several ladies a good deal of attention; one in particular attracted his particular notice, so much so, that the lady in question felt annoyed at him. Unfortunately "Dot" had partaken of several glasses of wine since the mishap with the brandy, and the consequence was that he began at last to feel muddled. About this time he happened to be sitting in a corner of the room in close conversation with the young lady to whom he had taken such a violent fancy.

"Haw!" (hic) he said, "what a lucky dog am I, to be in such an (hic) enviable position. What pleasure it gives me to be able to sing the praises of the Red River belles in their primitive (hic) loveliness! Ah me! I will represent them on the banks of the winding streams—their wigwams beautifully (hic) sit-situated beneath the noble, spreading branches (hic)—Haw! My dear!" Here followed a huge wink, and then the loud report of a hard slap could have been heard across the room, and "Dot" realized, as well as he could at the time, that it was no joke making fun of the Red River ladies, for his cheeks burned and his eyes blinked from the effects of the blow administered by the indignant girl.

"There," she said, as she rose from her seat, "take that for your pains. It may not be very lady-like of me to do it, but it is thoroughly deserved by you."

From *"Dot it Down": A Story of Life in the North-West*
by Alexander Begg (1871).

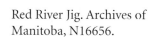

Red River Jig. Archives of
Manitoba, N16656.

WILLIAM FRANCIS BUTLER

My baggage was small and compact, but weighty; for it had in it much shot and sporting gear for perspective swamp and prairie work at wild duck and sharp-tailed grouse. I carried arms available against man and beast—a Colt's six-shooter and a fourteen-shot repeating carbine, both light, good, and trusty; excellent weapons when things came to a certain point, but useless before that point is reached.

Now, amidst perplexing prospects and doubtful expedients, one course appeared plainly prominent; and that was—that there should be no capture by Riel. The baggage and the sporting gear might go, but, for the rest, I was bound to carry myself and my arms, together with my papers and a dog, to the Lower Fort and the English Settlement. Having decided on this course, I had not much time to lose in putting it into execution. I packed my things, loaded my arms, put some extra ammunition into pocket, handed over my personal effects into the safe custody of the captain, and awaited whatever might turn up.

When these preparations were completed, I had still an hour to spare. There happened to be on board the same boat as passenger a gentleman whose English proclivities had marked him during the late disturbances at Red River as a dangerous opponent to M. Riel, and who consequently had forfeited no small portion of his liberty and his chattels. The last two days had made me acquainted with his history and opinions, and knowing that he could supply the want I was most in need of—a horse—I told him the plan I had formed for evading M. Riel, in case his minions should attempt my capture. This was to pass quickly from the steamboat on its reaching the landing-place and to hold my way across the country in the direction of the Lower Fort, which I hoped to reach before daylight. If stopped, there was but one course to pursue—to announce name and profession, and trust to the Colt and sixteen-shooter for the rest. My new

SIR WILLIAM FRANCIS BUTLER (1838–1910) was a lieutenant with the 69th Regiment, part of Wolseley's Red River expedition. He was their advance scout (spy) and wrote this journal as an account of his trip from eastern Canada to Fort Garry and the village of Winnipeg. He was an enormous man, something of a disadvantage for a spy, though he seems to have been successful. His later journals were written as he travelled to report on the smallpox epidemic in the west, going as far as Rocky Mountain House, 1870–71. In 1872–73 he made a journey to Lake Athabaska and on to Victoria via the Peace River area.

acquaintance, however, advised a change of programme, suggested by his knowledge of the locality.

At the point of junction of the Assiniboine and Red Rivers the steamer, he said, would touch the north shore. The spot was only a couple of hundred yards distant from Fort Garry, but it was sufficient in the darkness to conceal any movement at that point; we would both leave the boat and, passing by the flank of the fort, gain the village of Winnipeg before the steamer would reach her landing-place; he would seek his home and, if possible, send a horse to meet me at the first wooden bridge upon the road to the Lower Fort. All this was simple

Louis Riel and Council. Archives of Manitoba, N5396.

10

enough, and supplied me with that knowledge of the ground which I required.

It was now eleven o'clock p.m., dark but fine. With my carbine concealed under a large coat, I took my station near the bows of the boat, watching my companion's movements. Suddenly the steam was shut off, and the boat began to round from the Red River into the narrow Assiniboine. A short distance in front appeared lights and figures moving to and fro along the shore—the lights were those of Fort Garry, the figures those of Riel, O'Donoghue, and Lepine, with a strong body of guards.

A second more, and the boat gently touched the soft mud of the north shore. My friend jumped off to the beach; dragging the pointer by chain and collar after me, I, too, sprang to the shore just as the boat began to recede from it. As I did so, I saw my companion rushing up a very steep and lofty bank. Much impeded by the arms and dog, I followed him up the ascent and reached the top. Around stretched a dead black level plain, on the left the fort, and figures were dimly visible about 200 yards away. There was not much time to take in all this, for my companion, whispering me to follow him closely, commenced to move quickly along an irregular path which led from the river bank. In a short time we had reached the vicinity of a few straggling houses whose white walls showed distinctly through the darkness; this he told me, was Winnipeg. Here was his residence, and here we were to separate. Giving me a few hurried directions for further guidance, he pointed to the road before me as a starting-point, and then vanished into the gloom. For a moment I stood at the entrance of the little village half-irresolute what to do. One or two houses showed lights in single windows, behind gleamed the lights of the steamer which had now reached the place of landing. I commenced to walk quickly through the silent houses.

Continued

Messrs. Riel, Lepine, and O'Donoghue, surrounded by a body-guard of half-breeds and a few American adventurers, appeared upon the landing-place. A select detachment, I presume, of the "men not afraid to fight" boarded the boat and commenced to ransack her from stem to stern. While the confusion was at its height, and doors, &c., were being broken open, it became known to some of the searchers that two persons had left the boat only a few minutes previously. The rage of the petty Napoleon became excessive, he sacréed and stamped and swore, he ordered pursuit on foot and horseback; and altogether conducted himself after the manner of rum-drunkenness and despotism based upon ignorance and "straight drinks."

All sorts of persons were made prisoners upon the spot. My poor companion was seized in his house twenty minutes after he had reached it, and being hurried to the boat, was threatened with instant hanging. Where had the stranger gone to? And who was he? He had asserted himself to belong to Her Majesty's Service, and he had gone to the Lower Fort.

"After him!" screamed the President; "bring him in dead or alive."

So some half-dozen men, half-breeds and American filibusters, started out in pursuit. It was averred that the man who left the boat was of colossal proportions, that he carried arms of novel and terrible construction, and, more mysterious still, that he was closely followed by a gigantic dog.

People shuddered as they listened to this part of the story—a dog of gigantic size! What a picture, this immense man and that immense dog stalking through the gloom-wrapped prairie, goodness knows where! Was it to be wondered at, that the pursuit, vigorously though it commenced, should have waned faint as it reached the dusky prairie and left behind the neighbourhood and the habitations of men?

From *The Great Lone Land: A Narrative of Travel and Adventure in the North-West of America* by William Francis Butler (1879).

MARY AGNES FITZGIBBON

MARY AGNES FITZGIBBON was born June 18, 1851. In 1882 she married Clare Valentine Fitzgibbon. They had one daughter, Agnes Florence Frances Louise Fitzgibbon. Mary Agnes wrote a weekly article called "Driftwood" for the *Toronto Globe* under the pseudonym "Lally Bernard." She wrote a biography of her father, *A Veteran of 1812, The Life of James Fitzgibbon* (1894). She was related to Catherine Parr Traill, and edited or contributed to two of her books, *Cot and Cradle Stories* (1895) and *Pearls and Pebbles, or, Notes of an Old Naturalist* (1894). *A Trip to Manitoba* was published in 1880. She founded the Women's Historical Society of Toronto. She died May 17, 1915.

The Hudson's Bay Company's store had a great attraction for me. It was a long, low building within the precincts of Fort Garry, stocked with everything either useful or ornamental from a ship's anchor to a lace pocket-handkerchief; a sort of curiosity shop of all the necessaries and luxuries of life; an outfitting establishment where one could not only clothe oneself from head to foot, but furnish one's house from attic to cellar, at very reasonable prices. Whatever the charges may be at the outlaying posts, competition keeps them within bounds in Winnipeg. As a rule the goods are excellent in quality, and to judge by the number of carts, carriages, and saddle-horses always grouped about the door of the store, a thriving business is done there.

The Red River at Winnipeg is much wider than at any other point, yet so high are the banks, that until quite close to it, one cannot see the water. On the opposite or western shore is St. Boniface, the terminus of the branch line from Selkirk, and the site of the Roman Catholic cathedral, convents, and schools. The cathedral, a large square building, has a musical chime of bells, and the ringing of the "angelus," whose sound floated over the prairie unmarred by steam whistles, factory bells, or any other of the multitudinous sounds of a large city, was always welcome. Nowhere is evening more beautiful than Manitoba. One instance in particular I noticed. The sun was setting low down in the heavens as in a sea of gold, one long flame-coloured line alone marking the horizon. In the south-west rose cloud upon cloud of crimson and gold, crossed by rapid flashes of pale yellow and white lightning, which momentarily obliterated their rich colours. To the south was a great bank of black thunder-cloud crested with crimson, reft to its deepest darkness by successive flashes of forked lightning. Immediately overhead a narrow curtain of leaden clouds was driven hither and thither by uncertain winds; while below,

Highland cattle at Silver Heights, Winnipeg. Archives of Manitoba, N845.

the prairie and all its varied life lay bathed in the warmth and light of the departing sun, throwing into bold relief the Indian Wigwam, with its ragged sides and crosspoles.

Squaws were seated round the camp fires, or dipping water from a pool hard by; Indians were standing idly about; droves of cattle were being driven in for milking; groups of horses, their fore feet tied loosely together, were hobbling awkwardly as they grazed; tired oxen were tethered near, feeding after their day's work, while their driver lay under his cart and smoked. Above the low squat tent of the half-breed, there rose the brown-roofed barracks, its lazy flag clinging to the staff. Through the surrounding bushes water gleamed here and there. In the distance could be seen long trains of ox-carts, coming from remote settlements, the low monotonous moan of their ungreased wheels making a weird accompaniment to the muttering thunder; or a black-robed procession of nuns, on their way to the small chapel on the prairie, whose tinkling bell was calling them to prayers. An Indian on his fiery little steed, his beaded saddle-cloth glistening in the sun, was galloping in mad haste over the grass, away to the low hills to the north, which deserved their name of Silver Heights as they received the sun's good-night kiss.

Then the clouds, losing their borrowed tints, closed in like a pall; the low wail of the wind grew louder as it approached and swept them away to the south, leaving night to settle down upon the dwellers of the prairie city, starlit and calm, while the distant glow of the prairie fires rose luridly against the eastern sky. But all night long the creaking moan of the ox-carts went on, giving the prairie a yet closer resemblance to "an inland sea."

Continued

The 25th of April was a warm day, succeeding heavy rains, and it was hoped that the ice would move next day. In the evening we were at our assembly in the town-hall, which is built on the side of a broad, shallow *coolé* or gully. About ten o'clock, seeing several people look anxiously from the windows, we went to inquire the cause, and found the "water was out." Freshets from the prairies were rushing down the *coolé* beneath, carrying everything before them—dog-kennels, logs, broken furniture, boxes, and all the usual *débris* found scattered about the houses on the prairie. The freshets increased so rapidly, that it was feared if we did not leave at once we should never get home, the water being level with the bridge, which was in imminent danger of being carried away. The lower story of the hall was also flooded, and considered scarcely safe. So there was cloaking in hot haste, and the gentlemen who lived near brought all the top-boots and galoshes they could collect for the benefit of those who had to cross the partially submerged roads.

The ice did not move next day, and on the 27th, at the sound of the steamboat whistle, I ran to the window. As if by one impulse, every door on the main street opened, and the inmates poured forth, men putting on their coats, women their bonnets, while holding the kicking, struggling bare-headed babies they had snatched up in their haste to reach the landing as soon as the boat; boys of all sizes, ages, and descriptions, gentle and simple, rich and poor, mustered as though by magic. In five minutes the streets and banks of the river were black with people rushing to meet the steamer, and the shout that greeted her at the wharf was loud and genuine. It was the last time her arrival caused such excitement, as before another season the railway was running to St. Boniface, and freight and passengers could get to Winnipeg all through the winter.

The spring of 1877 was wet and backward, and we looked forward to our journey out to the contract, where a house was nearly ready for us, with anything but unmixed pleasure. In the hope that the state of the roads might improve, we delayed our departure until the first week of June. For my own part, I rejoiced over every additional delay, as I was loath to leave Winnipeg, and the many kind friends I had made there.

From *A Trip to Manitoba* by Mary Agnes Fitzgibbon (1880).

FREEZE UP. What is known as the Freeze up is that period of the year when frost, snow and ice have put an end to the nearly all outdoor work and closed up the rivers for navigation. Since 1888 the earliest freeze up of the Red River at Winnipeg was November 3, in 1910, and the latest opening on April 23, in 1904. The latest freeze up of the Red River was December 3, 1899, and the earliest opening March 20, 1910.

From *Western Canadian Dictionary and Phrasebook* (1913).

Dock scene at Fort Garry. Archives of Manitoba, N3440.

JOHN McDOUGALL

JOHN McDOUGALL was born in 1842 in Sydenham, Upper Canada. His father, George McDougall, was a Methodist missionary and, as a result, John attended mission schools and learned to speak Ojibwa and Cree. Like his father, he became a missionary. In 1864 he married Abigail Steinhauer. She died in the small-pox epidemic of 1870–71 and he later married Elizabeth Boyd. In 1873 they established a mission at Morley, on the banks of the Bow River. Throughout his life, he was involved with relationships between Aboriginals and the government, and took part in the negotiation of Treaty 6 and Treaty 7. He ran unsuccessfully for parliament as a liberal. He died in Calgary in 1917.

In the course of my business I was in Old Fort Garry a number of times. I saw St. Boniface, then a very small place, just across the river, and the home of Bishop Tache. I was in and out of the five or six houses which then formed the nucleus of the little village called Winnipeg. I rode frequently through the parish of St. John's, passing the house of Bishop Anderson, the Anglican head of Rupert's Land. I went down into Kildonan and spent a night in the home of the Rev. Dr. Black, who was one of father's dear friends. I also met there the Rev. Mr. Nisbet, who later on founded the mission work at Prince Albert. I visited some of the original Scotch settlers, and was looked upon by the elders as a degenerate, because, as they expressed it, "She couldna spoket the Gaelic." I spent two Sundays in this settlement, hearing Dr. Black the first Sunday, and remember thinking that this fine Gospel sermon was "broad" in more senses than one. The next Sabbath I worshipped with the Anglicans, and heard the Rev. Henry Cochrane preach an eloquent and inspiring sermon, and was glad that a genuine native had reached such a position. I have often felt sorry that the men who were instrumental in raising him to this height of development did not themselves keep ahead sufficiently in example, as well as in precept, but by their failure caused their weaker brother to offend, and later on to fall terribly from his high estate.

It has taken many centuries of progressive development to give a

Rev. John Black.
Archives of
Manitoba, N14623.

The first St. John's Church and Mission School, built by John West. Archives of Manitoba, N13806.

very small percentage of the stronger races of men the will power and ability to understand and observe the meaning of the word temperance. It is a very small sacrifice (if it may be called such), yet an essential factor with missionaries in their work with the pagan races, that they themselves be through and through transparent and consistent, or else to these will come the greater condemnation. But, not to further moralize, I will go back to the loading of my carts and the gathering of my stock, preparatory to my journey westward.

From *Saddle, Sled and Snowshoe: Pioneering on the Saskatchwan in the Sixties* by John McDougall (1896).

GEORGE YOUNG

REVEREND GEORGE YOUNG, DD, was born December 31, 1821, in Prince Edward County, Upper Canada. He was trained as a Methodist minister, and in 1868 came west to found the Methodist missions in the Red River settlement. He was involved in the Red River uprisings in 1870, as a sympathizer of John Schultz and the Canadian Party. He was present at the execution of Thomas Scott and he ministered to him at his death. Young returned to Toronto in 1883 and he published *Manitoba Memories* in 1897. Young died August 1, 1910.

In November, 1870, telegraphic communication with the great outside world was made to us a possibility, and the first messages sent and received were as follows:

Fort Garry, November 20th, 1871.
Right Honorable Lord Lisgar, Governor-General of Canada:

The first telegraphic message from the heart of the continent may appropriately convey on the part of our people an expression of devout thankfulness to Almighty God for the close of our isolation from the rest of the world. This message announces that close—as its receipt by your Excellency will attest it. The voice of Manitoba, uttered this morning on the banks of the Assiniboine, will be heard in a few hours on the banks of the Ottawa, and we may hope before the day closes that the words of your Excellency's reply, spoken at the capital of the Dominion, will be listened to at Fort Garry. We may now count in hours the work that used to occupy weeks. I congratulate your Excellency on the facility so afforded in the discharge of your high duties, so far as they concern this Province. I know I can better discharge my own when at any moment we can appeal to your Lordship for advice and assistance.

(Signed) "Adams G. Archibald."

To the above dispatch the following reply was sent:

To Lieutenant-Governor Archibald, Winnipeg, Manitoba:

I received your message with great satisfaction. The completion of the telegraph line to

Fort Garry is an auspicious event. It forms a fresh and most important link between the Eastern Provinces and the North-West, and is a happy augury for the future, inasmuch as it gives proof of the energy with which union, wisely effected of Her Majesty's North American possessions, enables progress and civilization to be advanced in different and far-distant portions of the Dominion. I congratulate the inhabitants of Manitoba on the event, and join heartily in your thanksgiving.

(Signed) "Lisgar."

Continued

Leaving Pembina, nothing special occurred until we arrived within four miles of Fort-Garry. On that day we fully expected to see the fort, and pushing on, were not a little disappointed, and perhaps annoyed, that a miserable piece of a road, in a neglected and miry condition, kept us back, and as night was upon us we were compelled to camp within four miles of the fort amid swarms of mosquitoes, and in a place that seemed very uninviting. In this there was a special Providence. About two o'clock the next morning, amid much lightning and thunder, a fearful storm of rain and wind, a sweeping tornado, came suddenly upon us. It was indescribably terrific—a real prairie storm, such as the 'oldest inhabitant' does not remember to have experienced before. Two tents were borne down by the first rush, and their occupants left without shelter under the pelting storm. Our tent was in danger of being run down by our waggon and buggy, which were driven by the wind right against it; but the Lord kept us in safety, and when the storm had raged out its hour we were all thankful to find but little harm done. And now mark the Providence. Had we reached the settlement and tented in the open prairie where the storm was more severe, our waggons and tents must have been destroyed.

We felt that the hand of God was upon us for good, and that it became us to bless His holy name for His continued care. On the day following, we crossed the Assiniboine by a ferry, looked into Fort Garry and Winnipeg, and then passed on to an encampment on the prairie six miles out, where the horses could rest and graze during the Sabbath. Thus have we been brought to our destination after a month's journeying from St. Cloud to Fort Garry.

But what a sorry scene was presented by that long-thought-of town of Winnipeg on the day we entered it! What a mass of soft, black, slippery and sticky Red River mud was everywhere spread out before us! Streets with neither sidewalks nor crossings, with now and again a good sized pit of mire for the traveler to avoid or flounder through as best he could; a few small stores with poor goods and high prices; one little tavern where "Dutch George" was "monarch of all his survey"; a few passable dwellings with no "rooms to let," nor space for boarders; neither church nor school in sight or in prospect; population about one hundred instead of one thousand as we expected—such was Winnipeg on July 4th, 1898.

From *Manitoba Memories: Leaves from My Life in the Prairie Province, 1868–1884* by Rev. George Young, DD (1897).

The execution of Thomas Scott. Archives of Manitoba.

THE RED RIVER VOYAGEUR

"Out and in the river is winding
The links of its long, red chain,
Through belts of dusky pine land
And gusty leagues of plain.

"Only at times, a smoke wreath
With the drifting cloud-rack joins—
The smoke of the hunting lodges
Of the wild Assiniboines.

"Drearily blows the north wind
From the land of ice and snow;
The eyes that look are weary,
And heavy the hands that row.

"And with one foot on the water,
And one upon the shore,
The Angel of Shadow gives warning
That day shall be no more.

"Is it the clang of wild geese,
Is it the Indian's yell,
That lends to the voice of the north wind
The tones of a far-off bell?

"The voyageur smiles as he listens
To the sound that grows apace;
Well he knows the vesper ringing
Of the bells of St. Boniface.

"The bells of the Roman Mission,
That call from their turrets twain,
To the boatman on the river,
To the hunter on the plain.

"Even so in our mortal journey
The bitter north winds blow,
And thus upon life's Red River,
Our hearts, as oarsmen, row.

"And when the Angel of Shadow
Rests his feet on wave and shore,
And our eyes grow dim with watching,
And our hearts faint at the oar,

"Happy is he who heareth
The signal of his release
In the bells of the Holy City,
The chimes of eternal peace."

Poem by John Greenleaf Whittier from *Manitoba Memories: Leaves from My Life in the Prairie Province, 1868–1884* by Rev. George Young, DD (1897).

Sketch of Turrets Twain from *Women of Red River* (1923).

R.G. MacBeth

"The French are off to drive back the Governor!" These words, somewhat excitedly uttered by one of my brothers, and addressed to my father, made up the first intimation I, a lad of ten summers, had that something serious was on foot; yet I recall the exact words as distinctly as if they had been spoken yesterday, and most of the acts in the drama of the rebellion whose actual outbreak they announced are indelibly stamped upon my memory. It was in October, 1869, and my brother had just come home from the morning service in Kildonan Church, over which upon that day the shadow of the situation had been cast, perhaps to the serious detriment of devout and undivided worship. The fact that the news first came to us in this way threw a curious sidelight on the primitive life of the time. The churchyard was the modern representative of the Athenian market-place, so far as the giving and receiving of news was concerned. The settlement had no telegraphic communication with the outside world; the solitary post-office was miles apart. A few of the people subscribed for an eastern paper, which was comparatively old before it reached its destination, and the local paper was doubtless often greatly at a loss for "copy." Moreover, it must be remembered that in certain seasons of the year the settlers were away from home haying, wood-cutting, etc., during the whole week. Saturday evening, however, they were all back. A general brushing-up was in order, and on Sabbath morning, except in cases of sickness or some similar cause, they were all wending their way in good time to the church.

From *The Making of the Canadian West* by Rev. R.G. MacBeth (1898).

Above right: Sketch of Kildonan Church from *Women of Red River* (1923).

REVEREND R.G. MACBETH was pastor of Augustine Anglican Church and the author of *The Making of the Canadian West: Being the Reminiscences of an Eye Witness* (1898). He also published *The Selkirk Settlers in Real Life* (1897).

JOHN BUNN

DR. JOHN BUNN wrote a letter to Donald Ross, the Chief Factor at Norway House, describing a great ball given in 1848 to mark the departure of the English military force that had been stationed in Red River. W.J. Healey quotes the letter in his *Women of Red River* (1923). Little else is known about John Bunn.

Red River, March 12th, 1848.
Donald Ross, Esquire
Chief Factor,
Norway House.

My dear Sir.

I am happy to find that notwithstanding the mountains of drift in which we are entombed, all communication from the outer world is not entirely closed. Such a winter for wind, snow drift and turbulence would induce one to believe that the Devil himself "rides on the whirlwind and directs the storm," or perhaps mother Nature is willing that only part of her children should enjoy the pleasures and frolics of the season, and likes to see the snow gyrating in the polka or rushing in the gallopade to the musical whistling of Old Boreas.

To describe the balls that have been and those that are to be is a task beyond the weakness of human nature. A mere enumeration would be a Herculean labor, but *the* ball is past.

Like the feast of O'Rourke,

"T'will ne'er be forgot
By those who were there
And those who were not."

My muse is not adequate to a description of all that was and felt on the occasion, but what I can I will do. The Patroness was in full bloom, radiant in silk and gold and gems of Ophir, her

Above left: Red River Belle, detail from Archives of Manitoba, Costumes Collection, 4, N8777. Full image p. 24.

face benignant like a harvest moon, as round, all smiles and perfection, except now and then the thunder-cloud of a threatened storm, but one cannot always expect sunshine. The room was most tastefully decorated with stars emblematic of those branches of the service stationed, and the motto of the Garter in each centre. Elegant festoons of evergreens were appropriately placed, and the orchestra was neatly ornamented with the Royal initials.

The amusements commenced by Dr. Duncan's choir singing a stanza of "God Save the Queen," and then "Here's a Health to All Good Lassies," and they further added to the enjoyment of the evening by occasionally interspersing some choice songs and glees, which were sung in a style hitherto unheard by the echoes of Rupert's Land.

Misses Caroline Pruden, and Margaret and Harriet Sinclair, were, I believe, considered the belles of the evening. Miss Lowman was held to be below, rather than above par, and this of course gave the gripes to Mamma. Polkas, galops, waltzes, quadrilles, cotillions, country dances, reels and jigs, employed the heels and talents of the assembly. There were cards for the infirm and lazy, brandy and tobacco for the thirsty, and unremitting hospitality to all. At midnight there was an elegant spread, consisting of all the delicacies nature and art could afford, to which ample justice was done.

At its close my memory expired. All became hiccups and happiness. Delightful, but indistinct, visions wrapped the senses in bliss, and a faithful version is lost to the world. Words are too weak to convey any picture of the heavenly trance, the strange mixture of celestial music, such as mortal ear never heard, and a medley of warriors and angels, mortals whirling, drapery flying, masculine legs fitting to feminine ladies. Now and then an ankle, small and clean-turned, would be crossed by a good sound piece of understanding, which if not appropriate to the Venus de Medici, would have done honour to a Mulingar heifer. I remember for some moments being enraptured with the contemplation of a cherubim, and imagination was gloating upon its fat proportions. A shake roused me. I found myself staring at the lady Patroness!

But such frivolity cannot endure. Next day brought headaches and recollections. I looked back upon the evening with pleasure, as it afforded unmingled gratification to the guests, and so satisfied the hospitable donors, and riveted the good feeling which ought to exist between the civilians and their very gentlemanly and kind military friends. It is not at all unlikely that some of the fair and lovely ones may suffer from scarlet fever, but none will perish. It, however, would appear that more than one has been bitten by a tarantula since. A few days ago Mrs. Mowat gave a fashionable ball and supper, and Mrs. Bird came out strong on the evening of the 16th inst. What took place at the Mowats, or what took place at the Birds, I am personally ignorant of, since having declined to be present at either, I must depend on the liberality of others. I love gaiety but I would eschew dissipation; where the line of demarcation ought to be made is of course a matter of opinion, but having reached my own, there I shall stop.

Had the parsons reserved their fire they might have preserved their character for good sense and maintained their pastoral authority; but they railed at dancing as a damnable sin, which no lady would believe, and now when they might say something about the abuse thereof, their ammunition is gone. They have fired a few pepper-corns from the pulpit about "Lot's Wife," "The Rich Man and Lazarus," etc., etc., but "'It is sparrow shot against a bastion,' quoth my uncle Toby." Papas may remonstrate, parsons may dispense brimstone by the wholesale, but the girls will dance. "Vive la bagatelle!" is the order of the day. But the fever will pass, reaction will come, and pensiveness and sighing will lower the dear little creatures down to the humdrum realities of everyday life.

We are looking forward with hope to a more favourable season. The abundance of snow gives promise of the lacking moisture. Should we be disappointed, there will be no recourse for us but to whet our teeth upon our live stock, and when that is gone, to live like pike in a pond. Of grain there is hardly sufficient to meet the wants of the lucky few who are holders; the masses are destitute of it, yet with the astonishing and flexible resources of this singular country, a remedy against starvation is found in the swarms of rabbits in and around the settlement, and the super-abundance of deer of various kinds in its vicinity. We are fated to be always embarrassed but never bankrupt, to feel the pangs of hunger but never the langour of starvation.

Remember me kindly to the ladies, young and old, and to Mr. Clouston, who is too happy to write to me, and I am too lazy to write to him.

Ever yours very truly,
John Bunn.

From *Women of Red River* edited by W.J. Healy (1923).

Social evening depicting evening dress. Archives of Manitoba, Costumes Collection, 4, N8777.

J.J. GUNN

The sun is set, and faint and far
The mellow church bells, wafting low
The call of peace to souls that war,
Make music in the after-glow.

Across the river's windings wide
The elusive echoes waft and float,
And faint and swell, and still subside,
Yet pledge a longed-for after-note.

And all the vibrant western sky
Is glorious now with golden haze,
A-glow to light for memory's eye
The hallowed scenes of olden days.

J.J. Gunn

From *Echoes of the Red* by J.J. Gunn
(1930).

View from Gunn's farm at East Selkirk. Image from *Echoes of the Red* (1930).

J.J. GUNN was born April 21, 1861, at the site of the present Lockport. His grandfather, The Honourable David Gunn, was a member of the first Legislative Council of Manitoba. John Gunn was a farmer and an apiarist, largely self-educated, but a student of the insects, birds, and flowers of Manitoba. He became president of the Western Beekeepers Association and was also a local postmaster and Justice of the Peace. He married Eleanor Flanagan, a schoolteacher, in 1905 and died tragically two years later, gored to death on his farm, at the age of forty-six.

The Hudson's Bay Company's officers were royal entertainers, and none knew better how to "celebrate" when occasion required; and down through every stratum of society their methods were copied, of course. And so all strove—and with astonishing success—to provide something good to eat and something fiery to drink, to entertain their friends on New Year. Those whose taste for the "ardent" was perennial and who lost no chance of indulging, provided accordingly; while such as never indulged at all still procured a quart or so to honour the day.

Even the Indians through the land, and their name was legion, remembered New Year's Day; none so well in fact; and long before sunrise were on the tramp, the men with their guns and the women and children with sacks or other receptacles in which to stow such gifts of food as might fall their way in a royal day's begging. It was the discharge of their "flint-locks" that usually aroused the slumberous white man on this particular morning. A visit from these people was always expected and prepared for at both farm-house and fort; and it was seldom indeed that they were turned away empty handed.

When a party of Indians came to a house they invariably discharged their guns before entering as a compliment to those within.

Another feature of their visit was that besides passing the compliments of the season and shaking hands all around they also insisted on kissing and being kissed. From this ordeal no one on whom they could lay hands was excepted, from the host and hostess down to the baby; the man-servant and the maid-servant and the stranger who was unfortunate enough to be within the gate not even escaping.

Any one who thinks he can take some fun out of New Year's Day, now, should just imagine if he can the comicality of the situation this custom was wont to produce. As may be supposed, few maidens were bold enough to dare an osculatory collision with an Ojibway brave, war-paint, feathers and all; and no more plentiful were the lads who could hold their ground before a wilderness of unwashed wrinkles and "wind-tossed waves of hair," plus unknown quantities, and minus, perhaps, an eye, nose, or a lip. So when a party of Indians entered by the back door, a common sight was a party of youthful whites making a hurried exit from the front, while the parents bore the brunt of the onset and feasted their dusky friends in the kitchen. But it sometimes fell out that this youthful rout encountered a second party of Indians at the front door, most effectually cutting off retreat and making confusion worse confounded. The bucks saw the joke of course, and dropping for

Sketch of dog team from *Echoes of the Red* (1930).

H.B.C. Hudson's Bay Company, and also irreverently said to mean Here Before Christ.

From *Western Canadian Dictionary and Phrasebook* (1913).

the nonce their proverbial stolidity—together with their guns and blankets—scrambled for kisses just like white men. That is, just like the white men of those days; for this custom of promiscuous kissing was one the Indian borrowed from his white brother and practiced side by side with him. Calling on New Year's Day was even more in vogue then, among both French and English-speaking people, than it is now and the osculatory form of salutation was always a chief feature of it. Another feature peculiar to the time was that one did not confine his calling to his own circle of friends. Calling was the thing to be done on New Year's Day, and when a party of young men started out they called on everybody indiscriminately as long as the day lasted, or their locomotive powers withstood the effects of the good things made or provided. They shook hands with everybody, kissed the girls as a matter of course, accepted or refused the refreshments as they felt inclined, and so moved on from house to house.

The New Year's dinner and the big plum pudding were for the family and invited guests, but hospitality was of a free and open sort, and if anyone dropped in while the meal was in progress, he was quickly provided with a seat thereat.

There were dancing parties too, though these were not confined to the holiday season, where "hornpipes, jogs, strath-peys and reels put life and mettle in their heels." Or perhaps it would be nearer right to say that they put life and mettle into the dances. In the healthful, vigorous society of the time, physical exuberance required vents, "and lo! There was a time to dance,"

and dance they did, as nobody dances nowadays. The difference between the Red River jig and the Blue Danube waltz is the difference between the bonny buxom lass of those pristine "hoe-it-downs" and the limp and lackadaisical belle of city "functions," who also, thank goodness, is going out before the bicycle girl and the bloomer girl, and the girl who wants to vote, bless them!

From *Echoes of the Red* by J.J. Gunn (1930).

Detail of the cast of Minstrel Show, Votes for Women, c. 1915. Archives of Manitoba, Foote Collection, N2721.

JANE ROLYAT

JANE ROLYAT was the pseudonym of E. Jane Taylor. Little biographical information is available for Taylor. She was the daughter of a Saskatchewan judge, and later married Neil McDougal. *The Lily of Fort Garry* (1930) and *Wilderness Walls* (1933) were the first two novels in a planned trilogy that was never completed. *The Canadian Forum* of September 1930 described her as the author who might become the Canadian novelist of major renown.

From one of his many journeys her father had once returned to Fort Garry in the middle of winter. On the last portion of a difficult and roundabout route, five hundred miles or more north from St. Paul by dog-sled he had travelled with the greatest vigour because of the severity of the weather; and because he had so much wished to be with them.

How he had relished his first meal at home, consisting chiefly of steaming rubaboo and bannock buttered with buffalo marrow fat. Not in all his travels had he tasted food more excellent. 'The pot-luck of the plains' he had declared was most satisfying.

After supper they had all sat around the big fire-place, the family and two 'Frenchmen' from across the river, whilst papa in his rich voice had told of wonders of the East, light from blazing billets falling on his face, on his luxuriant moustache, on his high twists of fair hair, one large curl seated above all as on a throne.

How fresh a manner he had of describing scenes of nature, and how fascinated they all had been by his accounts of adventures. Pierre and Antoine had taken their clay pipes out of their mouths and gaped. Pierre Collette who had led the hunt and Antoine Basson who had guided boats on long voyages. Both had been many times 'the plains across', but they knew nothing of the East, although their grandsires, papa had said, would have been *coureurs de bois* or *voyageurs* in Quebec.

How the frost, Margaret next recalled, had penetrated the night of her father's return, lurking in corners, around windowsills and doors, ready to dash into the middle of the room and take complete possession should the fire slacken for a moment. At times it had rendered vocal the timbers of the house so that it had seemed as if they might split asunder. Mamma and

Above left: St. Boniface Cathedral as it appears seventy-five years after Rolyat's *Lily of Fort Garry*. Photo by Ben MacPhee-Sigurdson.

Donovan had kept piling on more and more wood until its hot roaring and the icy reports from the logs of their residence were like two demons contending. And Pierre and Antoine, hardy as they were—at least tearing themselves away from the spell of her father's rich voice, triumphant over the combined voices of frost and fire—after having been treated amply to rum, had gone out in their wolf costumes into the sharp night, crossing themselves.

That severe winter little Tim had been born. Papa had brought Mistress Denny, carrying her outright part of the way, and her bundles, over billows of snow to the corner of the house, to the opening there.

It had been singular. She could see it yet, the snow blown away from the front of the house into a high wall, affording a clear passage. For a long time it had remained that way. It was curious. She could see it yet and that had been many years ago. Many years ago.

She calculated. Four years ago, in fact. A long time ago. Many things had happened since then. In that period her father had gone away three times and returned twice. In that period she had had four birthdays, making her now sixteen. Within that period she had completed her education at the Red River Academy, where she had been instructed in various branches of knowledge, including 'the use of the globe, rules of deportment, rules governing conduct,' and last but not least, 'correct speech with French phrases.'

A long time ago. Moreover in winter. Summer was now beginning after another winter, long, creaking and growling, as it had seemed to her, much in the house. It was now, one might safely say, summer; and indeed this day in 'the moon of young birds,' to use old Madeleine's phrase, had had several uncommonly hot hours and it was still much too warm. *Une chaleur étouffante*, in fact.

However (she bit her childish lips, recollecting all at once Number Three in Rules of Conduct) she should not complain. One does not complain. The weather was as it should be. It was a perfect evening and the sunset was most beautiful.

This resolved, and her lips chastened, though they had not moved, she continued to gaze out into the prairie with an agreeable expression on her face, imagining too—it was a good thought—that she saw the figure of her father in the billowy distance. She had no reason for indulging in this fancy. Her mother had not dropped the slightest hint. As likely as not it would be the middle of winter when papa would come, as before. However, one could imagine and it was a good thought.

So she stared ahead of her pleasantly and very intently, too, as if she might by force of eyesight as well as of imagination draw a solitary horseman forward to the settlement from out the depths of the plains, which truth compels it to be acknowledged, stretched before her in the exceptional hush of a great heat. The usual murmur of the wind in the long grasses was stilled. There was not the slightest breeze. Not a twig stirred in the smattering of poplars nearby. From the house and stable-yard behind her no sound came.

Was it to forget the heat, to assume with her Number Three in Rules of Conduct, to project only agreeable ideas, that all movement of any sort, human or otherwise, was being suspended while the dying sun drew over the vast tableau of 'the great lone land,' beginning with the Colony at its remote eastern border, a swift running flame of brightness? The eye of a bird might have seen its effect in its entirety; waters meeting within the Colony flashing into life, whitewashed homes along the banks among the trees, tinted pink below; windows of St. Boniface Cathedral at the confluence of the rivers burning as with an inner fire; across, the grey stone walls of Fort Garry, its bastions and black guns, and roofs of big rectangular buildings along the walls, all blocked out in something of a reminiscent ruddiness, that fluttered too on the flag above all, flag of Company and of country, that turned tents of plain Crees in the space allotted them near the Fort into a collection of rusty cones, that gave to the rough wood of a windmill standing out from among the trees the appearance of unpolished mahogany, that

Sketch of Upper Fort Garry. *London Illustrated News*, February 12, 1870.

illuminated, finally, regarding southwest from the Fort, to notice no more, Margaret herself, so that her fair hair became straightway a blushing halo—and then no more.

For it did not long endure, this last earthbound splendour of the sun; and other effects quite visible to her, which no doubt had assisted her in her creative effort, a lakelet sparkling under a film of rosy light, dark wine spilled into a hollow, the dazzling green of grass at her feet, soon dissolved. Yet she still gazed ahead as if in expectation, until the fiery red ball dropping from sight launched upward slanting rays that painted clouds in every direction many colours, until that great glory above fell in part to mauve, purple and slate blue ruins, until the whole prairie below lacked lustre and inspiration, until she could no longer see even in imagination of solitary horseman advancing; rather a mist rising from the ground and creeping towards her.

Continued

And there! Her attention swept suddenly to the end of vision. A surprise! If she had not been seated on the ground and established on the robe as she was established she could not, she was sure, have seen this touch of colour at all. An orange-dyed canoe, shooting into sight

RED RIVER CART. A primitive vehicle much used in the early days of settlement in the West. It was constructed entirely of wood, even to the wheels and axles, and, on the trail, emitted a screeching noise that was heard (so old-timers say) long before the cart itself came into sight.

From *Western Canadian Dictionary and Phrasebook* (1913).

and vanishing. A tiny shallop, in its vivid stain and in its swiftness a mere flash in a shining pan of water, but a most cheering flash. Margaret's eyes snatching at every crumb of glamour, brightened for the moment; then returned to the water nearer at hand and rested there once more softly glistening; again somewhat wistfully.

In the more populous parts of the settlement, nearer the Fort perhaps, there would be many such gaily painted boats on the river. In the absence of a bridge, 'dug-outs' as they properly were and a rude ferry were the only means of crossing in open water. On fine summer evenings they would weave back and forth in considerable numbers, shuttles, securing the basic threads of the Colony—Indian blood, in three fourths of the population of 10,000—irrespectively of creed or language. Strong little shuttles, weaving a friendly, an amorous, or merely a useful cloth.

From *The Lily of Fort Garry* by Jane Rolyat (1930).

Red River cart, 1871. Archives of Manitoba, N16063.

Buffalo Bill Cody & Métis at Upper Fort Garry, 1910. University of Manitoba Archives and Special Collections, PC 18 Upper Fort Garry, 18-5947-14.

BOOM TOWN WINNIPEG

"In between the rubber and silk markets and the Winnipeg grains there oozes a little of the fizz and sizzle of the Faubourg Montmartre."
From *Tropic of Cancer* by Henry Miller (1934).

Above: The Bawlf and Benson Block. Archives of Manitoba, Winnipeg Views/Album 3. Previous page: Princess Street. Archives of Manitoba, N4826.

DAVID CURRIE

Although I have not yet met with "croakers," I have met a good many of another class, whom for want of a better name I shall designate as

"PUFFERS."

These individuals hang around taverns and drink and swear like troopers, and are ready to assist immigrants when paid exorbitant wages for their services. When one of these puffers overhears an immigrant complaining of the excessive charges, or any other inconvenience arising from the people, country, climate, or water, Mr. Puffer begins to taunt him with cowardice, and tells him he had better go back to Ontario, as he is too much of a green-horn to get along in Manitoba, where he "will likely be lost in the mud or eaten up by mosquitoes." Some of the Government officials are of this class, and do more to disgust intending settlers with the country than almost any other thing I know of. I have on several occasions begun to complain of Manitoba in the presence of some puffer, just for the fun of hearing him rage and rave at the cowardice of "some people," which of course includes myself. In justice to the country, I must say that from all I have seen, it is fully equal to my most sanguine expectations, except in the exceedingly small amount which has yet been brought under cultivation, and also the large area which is at present under water (I should say under ice). The water has an unpleasant taste, but seems to be quite healthy, and the soil is such as would make almost any farmer's eyes sparkle.

Above right: Immigrants outside General Office, Main at Broadway, c. 1880s. Archives of Manitoba, N9724.

DAVID CURRIE was a journalist and a correspondent for the *Montreal Witness*. He was born on a backwoods farm in eastern Canada, and he cleared and settled his own farm. He set out as a correspondent to describe the "Manitoba Fever" that was sending hundreds of settlers to the west. His letters appeared in the *Montreal Witness* and were collected as *The Letters of Rusticus: Investigations in Manitoba and the Northwest for the Benefit of Intending Emigrants* (1880).

Continued

Most people in Canada have already heard of

MANITOBA MUD

But I think very few have any just conception of its friendly adhesiveness. Where there is considerable water along with the mud there is not much greater difficulty in travelling through it than on many of the roads in the eastern provinces. If the surface water is drained off the mud dries, with a bright sunshine, in a surprisingly short time, and the surface of the road soon assumes the appearance of some of the asphalt sidewalks in Montreal, being a little springy, and very pleasant to walk on. Last night we had a considerable shower of rain, and this forenoon I walked around the city a good deal to study the peculiarities of this black mud, which you can hardly persuade yourself is not mixed with tar. You don't need to get off the sidewalks to get your boots clogged to almost any desirable weight, as the wagon wheels gather up a cubic foot or two of mud each, and at the plank street-crossing the jolting shakes it off. It is taken up by the feet of travellers and conveyed to the sidewalk, where it is distributed along in curiously-shaped lumps ranging in size from

A MARBLE TO A GOOSE EGG.

In a short time the sidewalks in the most travelled localities become nearly covered with these lumps, which are ready to adhere to the first boot that comes along. If you happen to cross the street where there is no sidewalk you will soon have cause to repent your temerity. This morning I crossed the street at a place where yesterday I passed over what seemed to be a beautiful asphalt pavement, but today, although my boots did not sink more than half an inch, the mud soon rolled up on each side of my boots until the ascending mud walls met together on the top, or instep of the boot, causing them to look more

like a pair of mallets than anything else—the weight, also was not to be despised. When I reached the sidewalk, I succeeded in getting free from the greater portion of the superfluous weight by stamping violently on the hard boards, but a considerable portion would still remain, and required a good deal of scraping with a stick before I could proceed with any facility. Under these circumstances the

BOOT-BLACKS

Get a good deal to do, but they spend much more time in scraping the boots than in brushing them. It was amusing to see how the mud would gather on the tires of the wheels, sometimes creeping up the spokes until the hub was reached, and the wheel became nearly a solid black mass. I have been informed by several persons that even empty vehicles are brought to a stand-still on the street owing to the accumulation of mud on the wheels. Such mud accumulations are always worst on unfrequented portions of the streets and in places that are not very wet. The mud, however, dries up very rapidly, and after two or three hours of bright sun, the road which could scarcely be gone over becomes one of the most desirable that one could wish to walk or drive

COST OF LIVING. The following were retail prices at Winnipeg in March 1913: Bacon 25c. per lb., beef 14c., bread 5c., butter up to 45c., cheese 20c., coal per ton $11.00, coal oil 30c., coffee 40c., eggs (per dozen) 35c., fish, fresh, 15c.–18c., flour 4c., lard 20c., milk (per quart) 10c., mutton, 22c.–25c., pork (salt) 20c., potatoes (per bushel) 75c., rice 5c., sugar 6 2/3c., starch 10c., tea 40c., vinegar 15c., wood (per cord) $8.50, rent varies greatly. The rent of a house in Winnipeg of four to six rooms may be anywhere from $15.00 to $50.00 per month.

From *Western Canadian Dictionary and Phrasebook* (1913).

Main Street, west side, south from Thistle, c. 1880. Archives of Manitoba, N13801.

on. When at Emerson I chanced to get my feet rather muddy, and observing a lot of prairie hay lying near, I stepped on it and began to rub my feet on it, thinking to clean them, but the hay stuck to the boots, which began to look like hedge-hogs and I was compelled to go to a convenient log, sit down and disentangle them by the aid of my hands.

From *The Letters of Rusticus* by David Currie (1880).

WINSTON CHURCHILL

WINSTON CHURCHILL was born in Blenheim Palace, Woodstock, on November 30, 1874. He became Prime Minister of Britain in 1940 when Neville Chamberlain was defeated on a non-confidence motion. He was Prime Minister until the election of 1945, when Clement Atlee won a landslide victory. Churchill returned to power after the 1951 election but he was in ill health from which he never recovered and he left politics in 1955. He died January 24, 1965.

1901: MANITOBA

WINSTON CHURCHILL TO HIS MOTHER, LADY RANDOLPH CHURCHILL, IN ENGLAND

Canadians had rarely seen or heard a more dashing and captivating speaker than twenty-seven-year-old Winston Churchill. The British MP for the Lancashire riding of Oldham had caused a sensation in South Africa by his derring-do as both a reporter and a serving officer. He then crossed the Atlantic to cash in on his celebrity status with a North American lecture tour on the Boer War. The tour netted him £1,600, the equivalent today of about $200,000. By far the warmest reception he received came in Winnipeg.

22 January 1901, Winnipeg

My dearest Mamma,

Your letter and some rubbish in the American newspapers alarmed me a good deal with the prospect of another general election and another battle at Oldham which I really do not think I should . . . have had the strength to fight. Your cable and one at the same time from Captain Middleton reassured me that there would not necessarily be a Dissolution.

So the Queen is dead. The news reached us at Winnipeg and this city far away among the snows, fourteen hundred miles from any British town of importance began to hang its head and hoist half-masted flags. A great and solemn event: but I am curious to know about the King. Will it entirely revolutionise his way of life? Will he sell his horses and scatter his Jews or will Reuben Sassoon be enshrined among the crown jewels and other regalia? Will he become desperately serious? Will he continue to be friendly to you? Will the Keppel [Alice Keppel, the new king's mistress] be appointed 1st Lady of the Bedchamber? Write to tell me all about this to Queenstown. (SS Etruria leaving New York on the 2nd prox.)

I contemplated sending a letter of condolence and congratulations mixed, but I am uncertain how to address it and also whether such procedure would be etiquette. You must tell me. I am most interested and feel rather vulgar about the matter. I should like to know an Emperor and a King. Edward the VIIth—gadzooks what a long way that seems to take one back! I am glad he has got his innings at last, and am most interested to watch how he plays it.

I have had a most successful meeting at Winnipeg. Fancy 20 years ago there were only a few mud huts-tents: and last night a magnificent audience of men in evening dress & ladies half out of it, filled a fine opera house and we took $1,150 at the doors. 1,230 [people]: more that is to say than in cities like Newcastle. Winnipeg has a wonderful future before it. At the back of the town there is a large wheat field 980 miles long & 230 broad—not all cultivated yet, but which will some [sic] feed the whole of the British Isles. I called the town "Great Britain's Breadspot," at which

they purred. They are furiously British and a visit to them is most exhilarating. But of course you must have passed through on your last journey round the world. . . .

Always your loving son
Winston

PS. I have been reading "An English Woman's Love Letters." Are all Mothers the same?

Please send letters and complete files of papers—*Times, Spectator, Saturday Speaker, Punch* etc to Queenstown to meet me.

From *Canada: A Portrait in Letters 1800–2000* by Charlotte Gray (2003).

Winnipeg Opera House, c. 1900.
Archives of Manitoba.

VINCE LEAH

VINCE LEAH (1913–1993) was born in Winnipeg. He began writing for the *Winnipeg Tribune* in 1930 and was a sportswriter there for fifty years. He joined the *Winnipeg Free Press* in 1980 and also wrote for *Seniors Today*. Among his works are *Pages from the Past* (1975) and *Hoofbeats on My Heart*.

WHEN WE WON THE STANLEY CUP

Eyebrows arch and questions are asked when somebody talks about the time Winnipeg won The Stanley Cup, emblematic of world hockey supremacy.

How did they get into the National Hockey league and when, asks the younger set, which only knows that the historic trophy is competed for each spring by the top teams in hockey's major group.

What they do not know unless they peruse old record books or listen to their elders is Lord Stanley's battered gift was hockey's original trophy, a challenge event conducted by trustees in Ottawa to be contended for by any club in Canada that felt it was good enough to win it.

Lord Stanley of Preston arrived in Ottawa in 1888 to represent the Crown as governor-general. Lord Stanley was just one of the vice-regal representatives in Canadian history who was a sports buff.

He loved horse-racing, cricket and soccer but when he had his first look at ice hockey he was sold, hook, line and sinker on the winter pastime. Not only did he support the existing Ottawa club of the day, but he built a large outdoor rink at Rideau Hall and consented to the formation of the Government House hockey team known as The Rideau Rebels.

In 1892, after his return to England, he donated the trophy which remains the most-sought prize in hockey. Lord Stanley never had a chance to see his cup being contended for, but it appears he never lost his love for the game.

1896 Stanley Cup Champions, the Winnipeg Victorias Hockey Team. Courtesy Hockey Hall of Fame.

In 1895, the Stanley family introduced the game to Britain on a frozen pond on Buckingham Palace grounds. The palace team included the Prince of Wales (later King Edward VII) and the Duke of York (who became King George V).

Hockey is believed to have had its beginnings in Canada in 1847 where English troops were garrisoned, but there also was evidence that it was played in Montreal 10 years earlier. In 1890, it was firmly established in Winnipeg, and, in 1892, the first Manitoba hockey association was organized. Victorias, named for the Queen who ruled at that time, was the first club formed here, Winnipeg's was the second.

By 1896, Winnipeg Victorias were powerful enough to seek Lord Stanley's cup. To the great surprise of Eastern Canada the Victorias defeated their namesakes, Montreal Victorias, 2–0, to win the West its first hockey trophy. This was the era of seven-man hockey, no substitutions, pass onside and two 30-minute halfs. The Winnipeg team included Flett, Campbell, Higginbotham, Howard, Merritt, Armytage and Donald Bain, one of the greatest athletes in Manitoba sporting annals.

The Victorias' first triumph in Montreal caused tremendous excitement in Winnipeg. The Westerners were not conceded too much of a chance in Montreal. The Eastern team also objected to the referee, Alex Martin, Toronto, and asked for a postponement after the local lads were on their way east. The trustees denied both Montreal appeals although after the game *The Toronto Globe's* representative did not speak too kindly of Martin's officiating.

The Winnipeg club turned in a fine performance from all accounts. After 10 minutes of play, Howard fired the puck out of a corner and his team-mate Armytage rapped it home to open the scoring and a great dash by Armytage down the wing, the newspaper accounts said it even made his opponents applaud, led to the second goal, Campbell cracking home Armytage's pass.

The Winnipeg team ran into a plague of penalties . . . you were even banned for being offside in those days . . . and Bain was ordered off with Henderson of Montreal after a scuffle but the Western challengers were too strong on defence and apparently received superb goalkeeping from Merritt.

There was much joy in Winnipeg. The CPR Telegraphs had set up special wires to the Manitoba and Clarendon hotels and hundreds of people thronged the lobbies and awaited on the street for a report from Montreal.

Performances in local theatres were interrupted as the result was announced from the stage.

The Victorias were tendered a huge banquet on their return, although *The Tribune* editorialized that it would be unfair to their plain, ordinary work-a-day fans if as much as $1.50 or $2 was charged for the banquet tickets.

The Victorias were to challenge often for the cup after Montreal won it back in Winnipeg and in 1901 defeated Montreal again in a hectic series in the Eastern city. Henry Roxborough in his excellent book, *The Stanley Cup Story* writes:

"Winnipeg Victorias (who had lost to The Shamrocks in 1900) did not retire to hockey's wailing wall and mourn their loss. Instead they strengthened their team and just one year later in January, 1901, they again steamed East, determined to upset the Shamrocks."

Roxborough adds:

"The game was rough. Sticks on both sides were cut to razor-like effectiveness and in the slashing ankles were temporarily rendered useless. Players on both teams tried to see how near to the fence a man might be shouldered without being charged with manslaughter."

Winnipeg won this one, 4–3.

The second game was equally bitterly-fought. After a knock-down-dragout struggle, Winnipeg was in front, 2–1, and took the trophy home.

It is interesting to note, adds Roxborough, that Winnipeg's share of the gate was $5,600, no mean chunk of change in those distant days.

It is significant that The Stanley Cup, despite frequent challenges, came West only three more times after The Victorias won it for the second time.

In January, 1907, Kenora Thistles challenged Montreal Wanderers, the cup defenders, and defeated them in a two-game series in Montreal. The Thistle line-up included Joe Hall, Tom Hooper, Billy McGimsie, Si Griffis, E. Giroux, Art Ross, R. Phillips, D. R. Beaudro and the legendary Tommy Phillips.

Phillips scored all four goals in the first game and three in the second. However, the indignant Wanderers tossed a challenge right back at the Thistles two months later and regained the cup, defeating the Thistles on Winnipeg ice.

Griffis was to become captain of Vancouver Millionaires of the Pacific Coast league which had its origins in 1912, and lead the Coast champions to the cup in 1915. Seattle Metropolitans won it in 1917, but major league hockey in the West closed shop in 1926 and the players were sold to NHL teams.

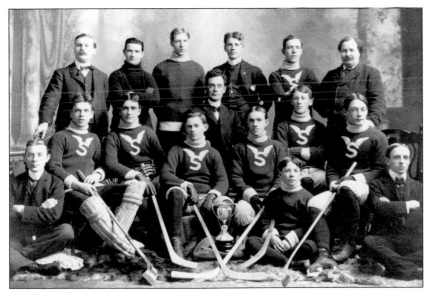

Winnipeg Shamrocks, c.1902. Archives of Manitoba, N3915.

ON WITH THE SHOW!

Sept. 30, 1891, was an exciting morning in Winnipeg's early history. Those who could get away from the shop or office were making tracks for the city's first industrial exhibition which was to stay open until Oct. 3. It was the first show of its kind in Winnipeg and the promoters, led by President Alexander MacDonald and C.N. Bell, secretary-treasurer, had worked hard to make it a success.

Winnipeg had long dreamed of an exposition, even if only a modest copy of the big fairs and exhibitions in Chicago and St. Louis and a well-attended meeting in city hall, Feb. 25, 1890, discussed the findings of a committee set up to investigate the possibilities.

A motion to ask city council to issue debentures not to exceed $30,000 for land and buildings was approved, but it wasn't until the following year that the exhibition became a reality.

A provincial agricultural exhibition was opened Oct. 4, 1871, but because of the threat of invasion by the Fenians, interest declined among the spectators. The United States army came across the border at Pembina and chased the invaders back onto U.S. soil—but that is another story.

The 1891 exposition attracted entries in agriculture, livestock, mining, manufacturing, horticulture, dairying and other lines. The main event as far as entertainment was concerned was "The Little World from Australia," billed as the greatest mechanical wonder of the age.

I remember seeing something similar on a smaller scale in a store window on Portage Ave. when I was a youngster.

The exposition included horse racing, pony and dog races for the children, a school drill competition, lacrosse and baseball matches, a dog show "covering the best and most valuable dogs in the country," band competitions, firemen's hose-reel races, military displays, children's races and athletic contests, the inevitable baby show, a printers' type-setting contest and "a magnificent display of fine arts."

General view of Exhibition Grounds, Winnipeg 1899. Archives of Manitoba, N9346.

Midway, Red River Ex night view, 1956. Archives of Manitoba, N1242.

Exhibition 1898. Archives of Manitoba, N9345.

The posters proudly proclaimed that the grounds would be lighted with electricity, and telegraph and telephone facilities were available in the event you wanted to let the folks at home know your pet Clydesdale had won the blue ribbon. The railways provided reduced fares.

Despite the unusual time of the year—fairs, generally, are held in the summer months and the promoters may have been risking autumn rains—the people turned out with great enthusiasm.

On opening day 65 rigs and 1,650 people were on the grounds by noon hour and, by closing time more than 7,000 had paid admission, a remarkable turn-out when you consider the city's size in those days.

There were more than 4,000 exhibits and the CPR, in a remarkable display of co-operation, had brought them free of charge from as far away as British Columbia. The provincial government had given the exposition a grant of $7,500 and city council had found 70 acres in north Winnipeg.

Civic-minded ratepayers had approved the bylaw for the debentures. Prizes for the exhibits totalled $13,500. Altogether, a stout effort by a rising young community. Winnipeg, you must remember, was less than 20 years old.

In 1892 the exhibition was held in mid-summer and, in 1904, it drew a total of 210,000 persons. The last exhibition was held in 1914 as war shadows gathered over Europe. That exhibition saw some firsts for Winnipeg, such as the first airplane. The big show was not revived until 1927, on the same site despite earlier efforts to change the grounds to West Kildonan.

The name Old Exhibition Grounds, remains. It is one of the better recreation areas in metropolitan Winnipeg with facilities for soccer, baseball, football, softball and hockey and, if there is finer turf anywhere, I have not yet seen it.

The 1927 show was successful. To a band music buff, the highlight was the visit of the Australian National Army band, a solid brass outfit highlighting Thomas Bollen, one of the world's outstanding cornetists.

But one rainy afternoon Bollen slipped on the boardwalk and sustained a nasty concussion. He spent exhibition week in hospital and did not get out to reveal his virtuosity until the band played two free concerts the following Sunday. I remember clearly the numerous encores whenever he stood up to play.

The depression killed the exhibition until 1934 when it was held at River Park in observance of Winnipeg's 60th birthday. Times were too uncertain to allow it to become an annual event again until 1951, when the enterprising young men of the Kinsmen club decided to sponsor a summer fair at Sherburn Park, the old home of women's softball, lacrosse and the baseball Maroons on Portage Ave. West.

In 1952, the Red River Exhibition was first held at Osborne Stadium, which also has disappeared. In 1954 it held forth at Polo Park, now the site of a shopping centre, and, in 1955, moved into the Winnipeg Stadium and arena. The Winnipeg "Ex" kicks off the schedule for class A fairs in Western Canada.

From *Pages from the Past* by Vince Leah (1975).

ERNEST THOMPSON SETON

This was all I saw, and it seemed little; but before many days had passed I knew surely that I had been favored with a view, in broad daylight, of a rare and wonderful creature, none less than the Winnipeg Wolf.

His was a strange history—a Wolf that preferred the city to the country, that passed by the Sheep to kill the Dogs, and that always hunted alone.

In telling the story of *le Garou,* as he was called by some, although I speak of these things as locally familiar, it is very sure that to many citizens of the town they were quite unknown. The smug shopkeeper on the main street had scarcely heard of him until the day after the final scene at the slaughter-house, when his great carcass was carried to Hine's taxidermist shop and there mounted, to be exhibited later at the Chicago World's Fair, and to be destroyed, alas! in the fire that reduced the Mulvey Grammar School to ashes in 1896.

Continued

It seems that Fiddler Paul, the handsome ne'er-do-well of the half-breed world, readier to hunt than to work, was prowling with his gun along the wooded banks of the Red River by Kildonan, one day in the June of 1880. He saw a Gray-wolf come out of a hole in a bank and fired a chance shot that killed it. Having made sure, by sending in his Dog, that no other large Wolf was there, he crawled into the den, and found, to his utter amazement and delight, eight young Wolves—nine bounties of ten dollars each. How much is that? A fortune surely. He used a stick vigorously, and with the assistance of the yellow Cur, all the little ones were killed but one. There is a superstition about the last of a brood—it is not lucky to kill it. So Paul set out for town with the scalp of the old Wolf, the scalps of the seven young, and the last Cub alive.

ERNEST THOMPSON SETON was born in Durham, England, on August 14, 1860. His parents emigrated to Toronto where Seton studied art, winning a gold medal from the Toronto Society of Arts. He then studied in London and Paris. He lived for a while with his brother Arthur in Manitoba and became a naturalist, interested in studying and drawing animals. In 1892, he was appointed Provincial Naturalist to the Manitoba government. His best-known work is the collection of stories, *Wild Animals I Have Known* (1898). He died in Santa Fe, New Mexico, on October 23, 1946.

The saloon-keeper, who got the dollars for which the scalps were exchanged, soon got the living Cub. He grew up at the end of a chain, but developed a chest and jaws that no Hound in town could match. He was kept in the yard for the amusement of customers, and this amusement usually took the form of baiting the captive with Dogs. The young Wolf was bitten and mauled nearly to death on several occasions, but he recovered, and each month there were fewer Dogs willing to face him. His life was as hard as it could be. There was but one gleam of gentleness in it all, and that was the friendship that grew up between himself and Little Jim, the son of the saloon-keeper.

Jim was a wilful little rascal with a mind of his own. He took to the Wolf because it had killed a Dog that had bitten him. He thenceforth fed the Wolf and made a pet of it, and the Wolf responded by allowing him to take liberties which no one else dared venture.

Jim's father was not a model parent. He usually spoiled his son, but at times would get in a rage and beat him cruelly for some trifle.

The child was quick to learn that he was beaten, not because he had done wrong, but because he had made his father angry. If, therefore, he could keep out of the way until that anger had cooled, he had no further cause for worry. One day, seeking safety in flight with his father behind him, he dashed into the Wolf's kennel, and his grizzly chum thus unceremoniously awakened turned to the door, displayed a double row of ivories, and plainly said to the father: "Don't you dare to touch him."

If Hogan could have shot the Wolf then and there he would have done so, but the chances were about equal of killing his son, so he let them alone and, half an hour later, laughed at the whole affair. Thenceforth Little Jim made for the Wolf's den whenever he was in danger, and sometimes the only notice any one had that the boy had been in mischief was seeing him sneak in behind the savage captive.

From *Animal Heroes* by Ernest Thompson Seton (1905).

Wolf illustrations by E.T. Seton. Originally appeared in *Animal Heroes* (1905).

W.H.P. JARVIS

Plummer's Hotel,
Winnipeg, Manitoba
November 20, 1—.

My Dear Mother,

Want of proper food and the lack of any companion with whom I can exchange ideas has had a most depressing effect upon my spirits, and the last evening when I arrived here I was particularly depressed. Every man I saw seemed to be my enemy.

Leaving the station and walking up Main Street the wind was cold and raw, and flakes of snow were in the air. Everybody seemed in a hurry, yet all seemed in good spirits.

As six o'clock came and the crowds of girls came out of the offices and shops laughing and hurrying to their homes, they seemed to me to be my enemies. The boys snow-balling each other and shouting in the street seemed to aim their missiles at my sensibilities, and it would have relieved me to box their ears.

All was bright and full of life—I alone was depressed. And then I began brooding on why I was different from those I saw around me. I was educated—they were not. They were happy—I was not. I envied them their happiness. My education is the production of much time and money, yet it is useless. It teaches me to suffer rather than to bear pain.

The jingle of the bells on a passing sleigh is gay and strong in confidence. The clammy hand of Despair does not muffle the sound, but I turn from the sleighs to the crowd and the shop windows.

Above right: Original plate from *The Letters of a Remittance Man to His Mother* (1909): *Remittance man in prairie bar.*

WILLIAM HENRY POPE JARVIS was born on May 23, 1876, of New Brunswick United Empire Loyalist stock. He published *Trails and Tales in Cobalt* (1908), *The Letters of a Remittance Man to His Mother* (1909), and *The Great Gold Rush* (1913), which has been translated into Finnish. *The Letters of a Remittance Man to His Mother* is in an epistolary form in which the narrator tells of his progress from being an effete Englishman to a true Canadian pioneer. The Winnipeg chapters are particularly poignant. Jarvis died December 14, 1944.

In the stationer's window I saw Santa Claus with a tin horn in one hand and a Union Jack in the other. Both the figure and the emblem reminded me of dear old England—England and Christmas. The thought seemed to me a mockery—the diabolical inspiration of despair. The crowd continued to hurry past, and in its mass I continued to see signs of contentment and of happiness in the faces of souls obtuse and uncultured, yet their happiness and their contentment show that they are active units in society, which I am not.

The coldness of the atmosphere fairly gripped my heart, so I sought the warmth of one of the hotels. I entered what they call out here the 'rotunda,' and sat down in a seat near a coil of steam-pipes. Gradually the heat penetrated my body; my muscles relaxed, and a great contentment came over me. Here was warmth at least, and being warm my hunger did not press me so hard.

It was now the hour for the evening meal, and I heard the word 'dinner' spoken by the members of the crowd about me. One man asked another to accept his hospitality, and the other refused, giving an excuse. How I wished the invitation had been given to me!

A man flopped down in the seat alongside of me. His face was flushed and bore signs of too much wine.

'Fine night,' he said.

'Yes,' I replied.

'Cold.'

'Yes, very cold,' I answered.

'You're an Englishman?' he asked.

'Yes.'

'Thought so,' said he, 'a remittance man. Remittance men ain't no good for work, but sometimes they make flunkies and bar-tenders, or further West they join the Mounted Police. The Mounted Police is nearly all made up of remittance men, and there ain't no better force on the top of God's green earth. Say! Will you have drink?'

What effect liquor would have in my famished condition I did not know, but I said 'Yes,' and went into the bar and asked for a glass of port wine. My host called for whisky, and drank liberally. As he drank he looked at me a long time, and asked, 'Remittances coming regularly?'

I replied that the Governor had refused to send me any more money, to which my new friend replied: 'He does right. If you're any good, you'll make your own way in this country. Been eating regular lately?'

I was first inclined to resent the question, but as the fellow seemed good-natured, I answered that I had had nothing to eat since early morning.

'Better come and eat with me,' he said.

This was evidently an invitation to dinner, and I replied that I would be glad to do so.

He led the way to the dining-room, and we sat down.

The immediate prospect of a good meal to be eaten in comfort caused a glow to pass through my body. As I took my soup the stimulation of the atmosphere outside, which had lately benumbed me, came upon me, and I felt the hilarity that had lately appealed to me as almost diabolic in the throng outside.

My friend ate and talked, and did each in an erratic manner. He said to me: 'You're going to try and get a job?'

I replied that I was.

'Well, then,' he said, 'let me give you a pointer. Chuck those pants you have on'—pointing to my riding-breeches—'and put on a pair of white man's pants, and your chances will be better.'

I told him that these were the only garments of this nature I had with me, the main part of my wardrobe being in the country.

'Well,' he replied, 'as soon as you get the money buy a cheap pair of pants, and your chances of success will be better. With those things you have on a man could spot you for a remittance man a mile off, and being a remittance man ain't the best recommendation on top of the earth for a job in which you are to make yourself useful.'

Original Frontispiece plate from *The Letters of a Remittance Man to His Mother* (1909).

As the fellow was talkative, and as they say only drunken men and fools tell the truth, I thought that here was an opportunity to gain the truth. My friend was drunk—he was not a fool—so I asked him what objection people had to remittance men, that they would not employ them. He jumped in his chair, and brought his fist down on the table so that the glasses rattled. His eyes shone out, and he stared at me.

'Why don't they give remittance men jobs?' he repeated. 'They don't give remittance men jobs because they are no d— good. They are no good before their parents send them out to this country to get rid of them. They can't make a living in a country where they are used to the ways, and yet they expect to make things go here, where they don't know the ways—and they don't seem to want to know the ways. If they did you'd get rid of those pants. Why are the remittance men no good at home? For the simple reason they ain't taught to be. From asking questions, the way I size the proposition up is that the remittance man is kept "lally-gaggin" round home doing nothing but making himself look pretty until he is twenty or twenty-two, and then his people come down to earth and find that it is about time he was earning a dollar or two for himself, especially as he is cutting up mean. Then they pack him off to Canada to become the free and independent gentleman farmer. They tell him to be sure and be a gentleman, and he generally is, for being a gentleman is to have the ability to borrow money on your face, when you don't know how in the devil you are to pay it back, and care less. That is why I never lend money to a remittance man, for the remittance men are mostly gentlemen. No, sir,' my host continued, and he got more excited. 'I don't want any remittance men working for me. They are a class of fellows who ain't been brought up like me. They have never been turned loose and made to rustle round at sixteen years of age, and their ideas of making themselves useful—well, they ain't got any ideas on the subject at all. It ain't because they are English that they're not good: it's because of the training they get in England, or the training they don't get—take it as you like it. Look at me. I rustled round the farm back east when I was nine years old, going to school in winter, and I got all the schooling that was good for me in the winter, and I've got a store up the line with a few hundred acres of wheat land and some cattle on the plains further west. I've earned them all, and how to ask a man for a loan of a $5 bill I don't know.'

'Give me the opportunity and I will make money.'

'Give you the opportunity! give you money! No, sir; the opportunity is here, right round you; but you've got to lay hold of it yourself, and before you can lay hold of it you've got to see it; therefore, young fellow, learn to size up your fellow-man. Don't be ashamed that you are alive, or ashamed to let the world see you alive. And be honest above all things—be honest; no matter how hungry you get, stay straight. You can shake yourself clear of hard luck, but dishonesty sticks like a mortgage on a widow's farm. It's worse than whisky is with me, and it ain't my fault I'm drunk now.'

Soon after this we finished our dinner, and my friend left, and I and my thoughts were again close companions. I left the hotel and walked out into the night. The stars stood out as glittering points in inky blackness, giving promise of greater cold. But I soon gravitated back to this hotel, and have passed the hours far into the night writing this letter. How I shall pass the remaining hours of the night I know not. Hunger is a great stimulus to thought, and it is probably because I have been thinking of what my host of the evening said during dinner that has made his ideas part of this letter. One thing I have decided, and that is that there is something I lack which prevents me from entering into life where force of personality is the gauge of success. Or is it something I possess in excess—self-consciousness or what?

Pardon me for detailing my troubles so strongly, but setting them on paper seems to give a vent to too much thought, the inspiration of my condition. The problem which attributes leads to success has taken hold of my fancy, which was stimulated by the ideas of my erratic friend at dinner.

Do not be distressed at my experience: I feel that I shall yet come out on top.

Your affectionate son,
Reginald Brown

From *The Letters of a Remittance Man to His Mother* by W.H.P. Jarvis (1909).

REMITTANCE MAN. "A duke's son, a cook's son, or son of a belted earl," who "left his country for his country's good," and who receives regular remittances from home conditional on his keeping away from home. It is alleged that there are many such individuals in Western cities, and a stigma is attached to a person suspected of being a remittance man.

From *Western Canadian Dictionary and Phrasebook* (1913).

ROBERT J.C. STEAD

Dave had often asked himself where it all would end. He traced it from its beginning; from the day when he wrote his first "boost" story; from the hundred-dollar bill that Conward had placed in his hands. It was a simple course to trace; so simple now that he was amazed that only Conward and a few shrewd others had seen it at the time. It had begun with the prosperity of incoming money; the money of a little group of speculators and adventurers and the others who hung on their train. They had filled the few hotels and office buildings. Presently someone began to build a new hotel. Labour was scarce and dear; carpenters, masons, bricklayers, plumbers, plasterers, labourers, had to be brought in from the outside. There was no place for them to sleep; there was no place for them to eat; there were insufficient stores to supply their wants. More hotels and shops and stores and houses had to be built and to build them more carpenters and masons and bricklayers and plumbers and plasterers and painters had to be brought from the outside. The thing grew upon itself. It was like a fire starting slowly in the still prairie grass, which by its own heat creates a breeze that in turn gives birth to a gale that whips it forth in uncontrollable fury. Houses went up, blocks of them, streets of them, miles of them, but they could not keep pace with the demand, for every builder of a house must have a roof to sleep under. And there were streets to build; streets to grade and fill and pave; ditches to dig and sidewalks to lay and wires to string. And more houses had to be built for the men who paved streets and dug ditches and laid sidewalks and strung wires. And more stores and more hotels and more churches and more schools and more places of amusement were needed. And the fire fed on its own fury and spread to lengths undreamed by those who first set the match to the dry grass.

The process of speculation was as easily defined. The first buyers were cautious; they looked over the vacant lots carefully; weighed their advantages and disadvantages; the prospect

ROBERT J.C. STEAD was born in Middleville, Ontario, on September 4, 1880. His parents homesteaded in Manitoba in 1882. He began his career as a newsman, and wrote a poem on the death of the British soldier Kitchener, which appeared in newspapers around the world. He worked for several years for the federal Department of Immigration and Colonization. Stead's keen eye for the details of prairie life in such novels as *Grain* (1926) and *The Homesteaders* (1916) provides some of the most compelling descriptions of the prairies in the early part of the century. He died in Ottawa June 25, 1959.

of the city growing this way or that. But scarcely had they bought when they sold again at a profit, and were seized with a quick regret that they had not bought more, or earlier. Soon the caution of the early transactions was forgotten in the rush for more lots which, almost immediately, could be re-sold at a profit. Judgment and discretion became handicaps in the race; the successful man was he who threw all such qualities to the winds. Fortunes were made; intrinsic values were lost sight of in the glare of great and sudden profits. Prices mounted up and up, and when calmer counsels held that they had reached their limits all such counsels were abashed by prices soaring higher still.

And the firm of Conward & Elden had profited not the least in these wild years of gain-getting. Their mahogany finished first floor quarters were the last word in office luxurance. Conward's private room might with credit have housed a premier or a president. Its purpose was to be impressive, rather than to give any other service, as Conward spent little of his time therein. On Dave fell the responsibility of office managements, and his room was fitted for efficiency rather than luxury. It commanded a view of the long general office where a battery of stenographers and clerks took care of the detail of the business of Conward & Elden. And Dave had established his ability as an office manager. His fairness, his fearlessness, his impartiality, his courtesy, his even temper—save on rare and excusable occasions—had won from the staff a loyalty which Conward, with all his abilities as a good mixer, could never have commanded.

He had prospered, of course. His statement to his banker ran into seven figures. For years he had not known the experience of being short of money for any personal purpose. Occasionally, at first, and again of late, the firm had found it necessary to resort to high finance. This was usually accomplished by getting a bank so deeply involved in their speculations that, in moments of emergency, it dared not desert them if it would. There are ways of doing that. And always the daring of Conward and the organization of Elden had justified themselves. Dave

was still a young man, not yet in his thirties; he was rated a millionaire; he had health, comeliness, and personality; he commanded the respect of a wide circle of business men, and was regarded as one of the matrimonial prizes of the city; his name had been discussed for public office; he was a success.

And yet this night, as he sat in his comfortable rooms and watched the street lights come fluttering on as twilight silhouetted the great hills to the west, he was not so sure of his success. A gas fire burned in the grate, rippling in blue, sinuous waves, and radiating an agreeable warmth on the May evening air. Dave finished his cigar and stood by the window, where the street light now poured in, blending its pale effulgence with the blue radiance from the grate. He was a man to be admired.

From *The Cowpuncher* by Robert J.C. Stead (1918).

Nova Scotia Bank, c. 1909. Archives of Manitoba, N9733.

54

KATHERINE HALE

The story of "The Streets of Winnipeg" is told by Mary Hyslop in an interesting little book which shows us, for instance, why it is that in a flat country there should be a crook in Main Street. The river was the highway, and as the river bends the street takes on its angles. Main Street is a long trail, the outcome of a growth, not a laid-out town like the newer cities of the western plains. Portage Avenue is the oldest trail to Edmonton and the longest street in the World. In the early days it was travelled by ponies and the old Red River cart, a vehicle made entirely of wood, "which could be heard long before it came in sight." Notre Dame is of French ancestry, but Logan Avenue and the old Logan homestead have disappeared. This house marked the spot where the dead were laid from Seven Oaks. Here too Lord Selkirk stayed during his visit to the colony. Fortunately, the old Fonseca House still stands facing McDonald Street. The grounds harbour trees and lilac bushes, but the family of old Spanish descent live there no longer.

The very names of these streets are fascinating. One, changed to Elgin was formerly Jemima Street, after a famous hostess of the early days. And there is Colony Gardens, now Victoria Park, which was the centre of social life in the colony. South of Portage Avenue to the Assiniboine River lay the Hudson's Bay Reserve; so, naturally, its streets received the Company's names. History is also contained in the cross-streets south of Portage Avenue, Fort Street and Garry Street especially.

The half-breeds and the prairie wagons and the Royal Mounted Police. Later the railroad and the horse-cars and the problem of muddy streets. There was the Big Boom of 1881 and then the American invasion. Capitalists began to discover the Canadian West. Winnipeg was overtaken by eager days full of work, full of promise, full of enthusiasm. The golden tide had begun

KATHERINE HALE is the pseudonym of Mrs. John Garvin. She was born in Galt, Ontario, and educated in Galt and later at Mrs. Veal's School in Toronto. She studied in New York and in Europe. She wrote journalism for the *Mail and Empire* of Toronto and published several short stories and collections of verse, including *Grey Knitting* (1914).

to rise and to surge in as though driven by some mighty natural force. Great Britain came to realize that here was a vantage point. In twenty years the population rose from thirty thousand to two hundred and fifty thousand people.

In 1907, Rudyard Kipling, speaking before the Canadian Club, said: "I went away from Winnipeg for fifteen years, which in the life of a nation is equivalent to about fifteen minutes in the life of a man. I come back and I find the Winnipeg of to-day a metropolis. The visions that your old men saw fifteen years ago I saw translated to-day into stone and brick and concrete. Dreams that your young men have dreamed I saw accepted as the ordinary facts of everyday life, and they will in turn give place to vaster and more far-reaching imaginations."

"May one write of Winnipeg and not speak of the cold?" I asked her one-time daughter, Nellie McClung, who could never have written her stories of the border-land of the Great West anywhere else, and she said, "Yes—the casual visitor is sure to comment on the cold of Winnipeg winters. But those of us who have called it home think of the warmth of the people's hearts and the happy days and nights spent within its hospitable borders. When I first knew it there were no skyscrapers or picture shows or juvenile courts or votes for women, but it was a great city, a dim rich city to me. I wish I knew as great a city now. I would like to find a city where shop windows are as beautiful and the streets as broad as Winnipeg's were then, and I would go far to see it—but there aren't any, any place."

The Rev. C.W. Gordon, "Ralph Connor," has been identified with Winnipeg for many years as the minister of St. Stephen's Church. At Banff his early mission work in the foothill country brought him in contact with some of the characters that have made his books famous. "Black Rock," "The Sky Pilot," "The Man from Glengarry" and others, were written in Winnipeg.

From *Canadian Cities of Romance* by Katherine Hale (1922).

Nellie McClung. Archives of Manitoba, N7694.

Fort Garry Hotel, August 2, 1924.
Archives of Manitoba, N2567.

JAMES H. GRAY

JAMES GRAY was born in Whitemouth, Manitoba, in 1906, and raised in Winnipeg. He attended Kelvin High School, but quit after grade nine. He worked most of his life as a journalist, writing for the *Winnipeg Free Press* and other papers. He is best known for his social histories, including *The Boy from Winnipeg* (1970), *Red Lights on the Prairies* (1971), and *Booze* (1972). He died in Calgary in 1998.

The railway was flanked most of the way by a succession of warehouses and factories, a flour mill, a lumberyard, and the iron works. To provide access from the Sutherland side to the Higgins side of the tracks, the city had recently completed a subway which joined Annabella Street on the west with Rachel Street for the entire length and was selected as the locale for the new red-light district.

In all Winnipeg no other site could have been discovered which would have served that purpose so well. It was far out of range of sight or sound of the pulpits of the moral reformers, it was well insulated from the downtown business section, and it was easily one of the city's least attractive residential areas. One side of Annabella Street from Sutherland to the Red River was given over completely to the coking ovens, coal piles, cinder piles, and gas tanks of the Winnipeg Gas Company. Facing the gas plant were a dozen modest houses and several shacks.

Winnipeg harlotry had kept pace numerically with the growth of the population so that it now far outnumbered the housing capacity of Annabella Street between Higgins Avenue and the river. However, immediately to the east was McFarlane Street, which ran from the C.P.R. tracks to the river, a distance of less than 300 yards. By adding McFarlane Street to Annabella, the new red-light area would contain fifty houses. As that total was more than the estimated needs for the moment, it was decided to incorporate only the west side of McFarlane Street into the segregated area. Neither Minnie Woods nor Chief McRae seems to have considered the interests of the hard-working residents of either street, or the result of permitting a row of brothels to operate opposite respectable homes on the east side of McFarlane Street.

Minnie went off to spread the word among the girls, and shortly afterward she was visited by one John Beaman, a real estate agent who had been sent around by Chief McRae. Beaman

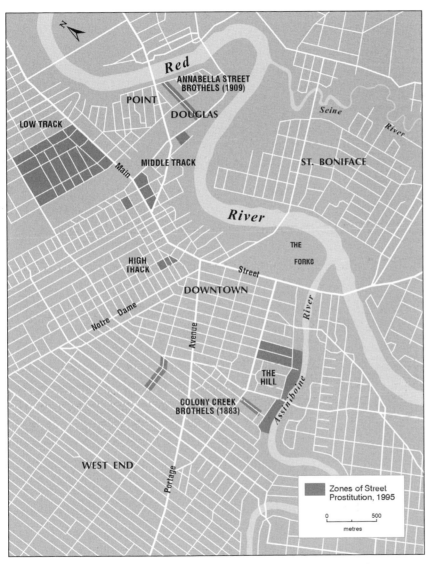

Districts of prostitution in Winnipeg over the years.

took Minnie for a walk down Annabella Street to inspect the houses. As queen of the whores, she naturally got first choice and selected No. 157, the largest house on the street, located midway between Sutherland and the river. It contained seven smallish rooms and had a broad verandah along the front. Beaman then conducted other women on similar tours and when he had a solid deal he approached the owners with purchase offers. He succeeded in buying most of the houses on Annabella for prices ranging from $2,500 to $5,000 which he resold to the women for up to $8,000. When word got around that a mysterious stranger was buying up property, prices stiffened on both Annabella and McFarlane streets. The late-comers, ergo, had to pay the stiffest prices. The highest price was apparently that paid by Lila Anderson, who was charged $12,000 for a double house at 113 McFarlane Street, which she claimed had probably cost $2,000 to build. Like all the other madams, she financed her purchase with a small down payment of $500 and whopping instalment payments of $225 a month. Rented to ordinary tenants the double house might have brought $30 a month.

By the middle of July 1909, Annabella Street was completely converted to brothels and McFarlane Street was perhaps a quarter occupied. But if the authorities had trouble from complaining citizens before the policy was changed, it was multiplied tenfold by the uproar that the invasion of the whores created in the Annabella-McFarlane enclave. Instead of the red lights in the windows which the Barbary Coast of San Francisco affected, Annabella Street went in for the largest electric porch lights obtainable and foot-high, brightly painted house numbers. Within a matter of weeks the new district was the most brightly lit area in the city. Soon the respectable McFarlane Street residents were being solicited as they passed back and forth from work. Their children were accosted en route to school. After the west side of McFarlane Street was filled with brothels, they began to spread to the east side.

Early in the fall of 1909 the police commission seemed to realize

John C. McRae, Chief Constable 1897–1911. Courtesy Winnipeg Police Museum and Historical Society.

that the existence of the April resolution on its books might lead to embarrassment if the complaints of the residents got out of hand, so it repealed that motion and thus left the problem of coping with prostitution up to Chief McRae on a completely informal basis.

The morality squad by then had put the houses under regular surveillance. The inmates were required to have a medical examination every two weeks and to produce medical certificates when required. In response to early complaints, Chief McRae decided that the brothel keepers were becoming a bit carried away with the light-burning. He ordered the porch lights removed and the house numbers reduced to normal proportions. Indeed, the morality department put a whole set of rules into force for the houses. The houses must not permit rowdy conduct on the premises. The women were not to go streetwalking, or embark on shopping excursions uptown without prior notification to the police, who sent a policeman along as an escort. There was even a rule that white women were not to be employed as cooks in the houses.

None of these rules prevented the behaviour of the inmates of the houses and their customers from getting completely out of hand. The residents of McFarlane Street became particularly vocal in their protests. As the opposition mounted, the police decided to back off a little by evicting the inmates and closing the houses that had become established on the east side of McFarlane Street.

On July 12 a Thomas Street type of raid was organized. The street was blocked off at both ends and the women were swept from one house to the next and then on to the next until they had better than thirty of them cooped up in the fourth house. The paddy wagon spent the rest of the afternoon hauling them to the police station, where the women cried foul at the top of their lungs. They had paid exorbitant prices for these houses on the understanding that they would be allowed to operate with impunity. They had good reason to accuse the authorities of double-crossing them. In any event, they pleaded not guilty and were released on bail. They were acquitted in the end and

RED LIGHT DISTRICT. That part of a Canadian city in which immorality abounds; also known as the cluster or hookshops.

From *Western Canadian Dictionary and Phrasebook* (1913).

their return to McFarlane Street signalled the complete takeover of the street by the brothels.

During the winter of 1909–10 relative calm prevailed and it began to appear that the city had solved its prostitution problem to the extent of hiding it away out of sight. But a wave of umbrage soon broke out louder than ever. When spring came, customers by the thousands swarmed into the new district. And not only customers. Winnipeg Sunday being what it was, the only available recreation for the populace was going for a stroll. Annabella and McFarlane streets became the mecca for Winnipeg sightseers on a Sunday afternoon. The women of the houses sunned themselves on their front steps, clad only in flimsy kimonos, and exchanged obscenities with such passers-by as spurned their proffered wares. As often as not, both streets were choked with hacks, taxis, and the hundreds of rubbernecks who milled about. They not only milled about the streets, they also patronized the brothels, as openly and casually as if they had been going in for a package of gum. A private detective hired later by the moral reformers swore that on one occasion fourteen Annabella Street brothels put through 292 customers in two and a half hours.

Not only was sex for sale but it is clear from the record that the brothels did a thriving business in bootleg in competition with the Main Street saloons. The delivery rigs of the wholesale liquor vendors hauled in Scotch and gin by the case and often by the wagonload. The brothels quickly became popular with under-age drinkers who had difficulty getting served in the licensed bars, which were under more or less regular inspection by the provincial liquor police. A recurrent complaint of the residents was about the number of under-age patrons seen emerging drunk from the houses of ill repute. The liquor laws of the province were enforced by inspectors employed by the provincial government, into whose jurisdiction the city police never intruded. The houses were all raided periodically by the provincial police, and the keepers pleaded guilty to violations of the liquor act and were fined $100 and costs. This was the minimum penalty for the same women appeared in court every three months.

From *Red Lights on the Prairies* by James H. Gray (1971).

STEPHEN LEACOCK

STEPHEN BUTLER LEACOCK was born on December 30, 1869, at Swanmore, Hampshire, England. His family emigrated to Canada in 1876. Leacock graduated from Upper Canada College in 1887. He received his BA from the University of Toronto in 1891 and his PhD from the University of Chicago in 1903. He taught for most of his life at McGill University in Montreal. Leacock is best known for his humorous sketches, including *Literary Lapses* (1910) and *Sunshine Sketches of a Little Town* (1912).

As soon as the province was established, everything moved with a rush. There was created a sort of economic vacuum and the air, an inblowing of men and goods, came rushing in.

Continued

So here was Winnipeg,—a little place of 250 people in 1870,—with its hands full and its beds overfull and its saloons more than overfull,—hammering away night and day to make houses, and clamouring for lumber and transport—and traders and adventurers and behind them, slowly gathering to a head, the rising wave of real settlers....The economic vacuum kept the little place at high pressure. Lumber that was worth seven dollars a thousand feet in Ontario sold for seventy dollars, coal oil, worth fifty cents a gallon 'back east', sold for five dollars 'out west'. No wonder the freighters could charge four dollars a hundred pounds for the Red River trip alone. It was,—in the 'economic' sense,—'worth' it.

That meant, if you analyze it out economically, that there was lots of money in Winnipeg to buy things and few things to buy, that there was the 'money' sent for the soldiers and the money for the government and the private money of the new traders and store-builders and merchants; and this means, after complete analysis of what we call 'money' and credit' that there were a lot of people in Winnipeg who had a 'claim' on the goods and services of the East and could say 'send me this and send me that': and the only trouble was to find the transport, the way to get it there.

No wonder things move fast in such a world,—where everything was young, everything to be done, and where everybody could make money out of everybody else,—nothing needed but transport, more transport, and more goods. These were the days when the railroad came into its own,—when people laughed and shouted and danced at the sight of the first train and loaded it with flowers, with the bell ringing and with merry girls riding on the cowcatcher! . . .

Things moved! Especially all sorts of 'first things'. The 'first' parliament met (1871) in 'Mr. A.G. Bannatyne's House', in the sitting room,—three entire rooms being assigned to its use, one upstairs and two down. The 'first oysters' came to Winnipeg in February 1871. In the same month came the 'first barber':

Continued

All this in the early days before the real 'boom' began. Measured statistically progress was slow. There were 250 people in Winnipeg in 1870, and 817 in St. Boniface and only 1,565 pure white people in all Manitoba. By 1872 the town still had only reached 1,467, but even in 1882, when all the world had heard of it, the population of Winnipeg was still only 7,900 and that of all Manitoba only a little over 60,000.

But the groundswell that indicated the tidal wave that was to come, appeared years before the boom in the high, the staggering prices paid for real estate

while the place was still little more than a hamlet. In 1872 the Hudson's Bay Company, so Grant tells us, sold as building lots thirteen of their five hundred acres about Fort Garry and received $7,000 an acre for them.

From *My Discovery of the West* by Stephen Butler Leacock (1937).

Wedding party. Archives of Manitoba, Foote Collection 1639, N15817.

General Post Office, Winnipeg, Canada.

General Post Office on Portage Avenue, 1920. Archives of Manitoba.

THE NEW CENTURY

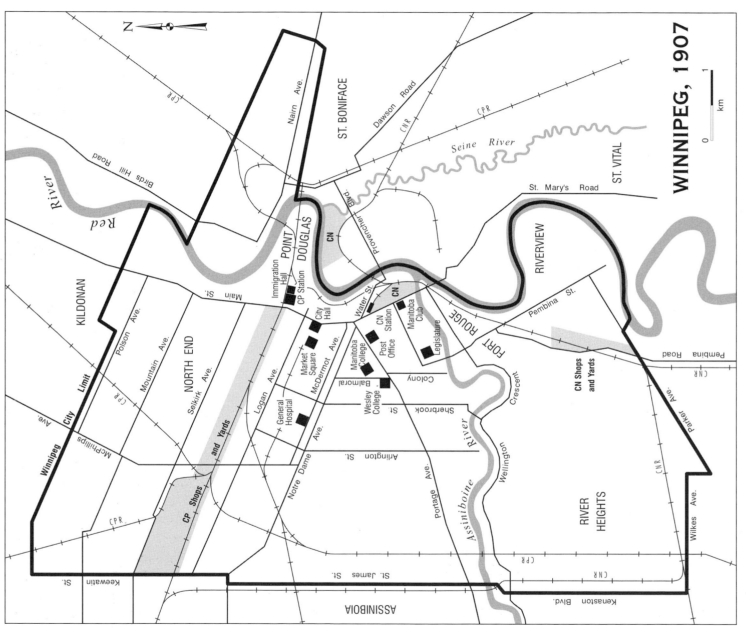

WINNIPEG, 1907

Above: Winnipeg, 1907. Previous page: Union Bank, Main and William, c. 1910. Archives of Manitoba, N1482.

RALPH CONNOR

Not far from the centre of the American Continent, midway between the oceans east and west, midway between the Gulf and the Arctic Sea, on the rim of a plain, snow swept in winter, flower decked in summer, but, whether in winter or in summer, beautiful in its sunlit glory, stands Winnipeg, the cosmopolitan capital of the last of the Anglo-Saxon Empires,—Winnipeg, City of the Plain, which from the eyes of the world cannot be hid. Miles away, secure in her sea-girt isle, is old London, port of all seas; miles away, breasting the beat of the Atlantic, sits New York, capital of the New World, and mart of the world, Old and New; far away to the west lie the mighty cities of the Orient, Peking and Hong Kong, Tokio and Yoko-hama; and fair across the highway of the world's commerce sits Winnipeg, Empress of the Prairies. Her Trans-Continental railways thrust themselves in every direction,—south in to the American Republic, east to the ports of the Atlantic, west to the Pacific, and north to the Great Inland Sea.

To her gates and to her deep-soled tributary prairies she draws from all lands peoples of all tribes and tongues, smitten with two great race passions, the lust for liberty, and the lust for land.

By hundreds and tens of hundreds they stream in and through this hospitable city, Saxon and Celt and Slav, each eager on his own quest, each paying his toll to the new land as he comes and goes, for good or for ill, but whether more for good than for ill only God knows.

A hundred years ago, where now stands the thronging city, stood the lonely trading-post of The Honourable, The Hudson's Bay Company. To this post in their birch bark canoes came the half-breed trapper and the Indian hunter, with their priceless bales of furs to be bartered for blankets and beads, for pemmican and bacon, for powder and ball, and for the thousand and one articles of commerce that piled the store shelves from cellar to roof.

RALPH CONNOR was the pseudonym of Charles William Gordon. He was born in Glengarry County, Ontario, in 1860. He completed a BA in classics and English at the University of Toronto and, after studying at Knox College and Edinburgh, he was ordained as a Presbyterian minister. In 1894, he moved to Winnipeg, where he lived until his death in 1937. His first novel, *Black Rock* (1897), was an immediate success and he published a long series of works informed by Christian values.

Group of immigrants arriving at the CPR Station, Winnipeg, February 23, 1927. Archives of Manitoba, N2066.

Fifty years ago, about the lonely post a little settlement had gathered—a band of sturdy Scots. Those dour and doughty pioneers of peoples had planted on the Red River their homes upon their little "strip" farms—a rampart of civilization against the wide, wild prairie, the home of the buffalo, and camp ground of the hunter of the plain.

Twenty-five years ago, in the early eighties, a little city had fairly dug its roots into the black soil, refusing to be swept away by that cyclone of financial frenzy known over the Continent as the "boom of '81," and holding on with abundant courage and invincible hope, had gathered to itself what of strength it could, until by 1884 it had come to assume an appearance of enduring solidarity. Hitherto accessible from the world by the river and the railroad from the south, in this year the city began to cast eager eyes eastward, and to listen for the rumble of the first trans-continental train, which was to bind the Provinces of Canada into a Dominion, and make Winnipeg into one of the cities of the world. Trade by the river died, but meantime the railway from the south kept pouring in a steady stream of immigration, which distributed itself according to its character and in obedience to the laws of affinity, the French Canadian finding a congenial home across the Red River in old St. Boniface, while his English-speaking fellow citizen, careless of the limits of nationality, ranged whither his fancy called him. With these, at first in small and then in larger groups, from Central and South Eastern Europe, came people strange in costume and in speech; and holding close by one another as if in terror of the perils and the loneliness of the unknown land, they segregated into colonies tight knit by ties of blood and common tongue.

Continued

"Who speaks for Jacob Wassyl?" cried a voice. It was Jacob himself, standing in the door, wet with sweat, flushed with dancing and exhilarated with the beer and with all the ardours of his wedding day. For that day at least, Jacob owned the world. "What?" he cried, "is it my friend Simon Ketzel and my friend Joseph Pinkas?"

"We were not invited to come to your wedding, Jacob Wassyl," replied Simon, "but we desired to honour your bride and yourself."

"Aye, and so you shall. You are welcome, Simon Ketzel. You are welcome, Joseph Pinkas. Who says you are not?" he continued, turning defiantly to Rosenblatt.

Rosenblatt hesitated, and then grunted out something that sounded like "Slovak swine!"

"Slovak!" cried Jacob with generous enthusiasm. "We are all Slovak. We are all Polak. We are all Galician. We are all brothers. Any man who says no, is no friend of Jacob Wassyl."

Shouts of approval rose from the excited crowd.

"Come, brothers," shouted Jacob to Simon and Joseph, "come in. There is abundant eating. Make way for my friends!" He crowded back through the door, taking especial delight in honouring the men despised of Rosenblatt.

The room was packed with steaming, swaying, roaring dancers, both men and women, all reeking with sweat and garlic. Upon a platform in a corner between two violins, sat Arnud before his cymbal, resplendent in frilled shirt and embroidered vest, thundering on his instrument the favourite songs of the dancers, shouting now and then in unison with the melody that pattered out in metallic rain from the instrument before him. For four hours and more, with intervals sufficient only to quench their thirst, the players had kept up their interminable accompaniment to dance and song. It was clearly no place for hungry men. Jacob pushed his way toward the inner room.

"Ho! Paulina!" he shouted, "two plates for men who have not eaten."

Continued

It was night in Winnipeg, a night of such radiant moonlight as is seen only in northern climates and in winter time. During the early evening a light snow had fallen, not driving fiercely after the Manitoba manner, but gently, and so lay like a fleecy, shimmering mantle over all things.

Under this fleecy mantle, shimmering with myriad gems, lay Winnipeg asleep. Up from five thousand chimneys rose straight into the still frosty air five thousand columns of smoke, in token that, though frost was king outside, the good folk of Winnipeg lay snug and warm in their virtuous beds. Everywhere the white streets lay in silence except for the passing of a belated cab with creaking runners and jingling bells, and of a sleighing party returning from Silver Heights, their four-horse team smoking, their sleigh bells ringing out, carrying with them hoarse laughter and hoarser songs, for the frosty air works mischief with the vocal chords, and leaving behind them silence again.

All through Fort Rouge, lying among its snow-laden trees, across the frost-bound Assiniboine, all through the Hudson's Bay Reserve, there was no sign of life, for it was long past midnight. Even Main Street, that most splendid of all Canadian thorough-fares, lay white and spotless and, for the most part, in silence. Here and there men in furs or in frieze coats with collars turned up high, their eyes peering through frost-rimmed eyelashes and over frost-rimmed coat collars, paced comfortably along if in furs, or walked hurriedly if only in frieze, whither their business or their pleasure led.

Near the northern limits of the city the signs of life were more in evidence. At the Canadian Pacific Railway station an engine, hoary with frozen steam, puffed contentedly as if conscious of sufficient strength for the duty that lay before it, waiting to hook on to Number Two, nine hours late, and whirl it eastward in full contempt of frost and snow bank and blizzard.

Inside the station a railway porter or two drowsed on the benches. Behind the wicket where the telegraph instruments kept up an incessant clicking, the agent and his assistant sat alert, coming forward now and then to answer, with the unwearying courtesy which is part of their equipment and of their training, the oft repeated question from impatient and sleepy travellers, "How is she now?" "An hour," "half an hour," finally "fifteen minutes," then "any time now." At which cheering report the uninitiated brightened up and passed out to listen for the approaching train. The more experienced, however, settled down for another half hour's sleep.

It was a wearisome business, and to none more wearisome than to Interpreter Elex Murchuk, part of whose duty it is to be in attendance on the arrival of all incoming trains in case that some pilgrim from Central and Southern Europe might be in need of direction. For Murchuk, a little borderland Russian, boasts the gift of tongues to an extraordinary degree. Russian, in which he was born, and French, and German, and Italian, of course, he knows, but Polish, Ruthenian, and all varieties of Ukrainian speech are alike known to him.

"I spik all European langue good, jus' same Angleesh," was his testimony in regard to himself.

Continued

"Suppose," agreed the Interpreter, "when Galician man get married, he want much joy. He get much beer, much fight."

"I will just be taking a walk round there," said the Sergeant. "These people have got to learn to get married with less fuss about it. I am not going to stand this much longer. What do they want to fight for anyway?"

"Oh," replied Murchuk lightly, "Polak not like Slovak, Slovak not like Galician. Dey drink plenty beer, tink of something in Old Country, get mad, make noise, fight some."

"Come along with me," replied the Sergeant, and he squared his big shoulders and set off down the street with the quick, light stride that suggested the springing step of his Highland ancestors on the heather hills of Scotland.

Just as they arrived at the house of feasting, a cry, wild, weird and horrible, pierced through the uproar. The Interpreter stopped as if struck with a bullet.

"My God!" he cried in an undertone, clutching the Sergeant by the arm. "My God! Dat terrible!"

"What is it? What is the matter with you, Murchuk?"

"You know not dat cry? No?" He was all trembling. "Dat cry I hear long ago in Russland. Russian man mak dat cry when he kill. Dat Nihilist cry."

"Go back and get Dr. Wright. He will be needed, sure. You know where he lives, second corner down on Main Street. Get a move on! Quick!"

Meantime, while a respectable Winnipeg lay snugly asleep under snow-covered roofs and smoking chimneys, while belated revellers and travellers were making their way through white, silent streets and under avenues of snow laden trees to homes where reigned love and peace and virtue, in the north end and in the foreign colony the festivities in connection with Anka's wedding were drawing to a close in sordid drunken dance and song and in sanguinary fighting.

In the main room dance and song reeled on in uproarious hilarity. In the basement below, foul and fetid, men stood packed close, drinking while they could. It was for the foreigner an hour of rare opportunity. The beer kegs stood open and there were plenty of tin mugs about.

From *The Foreigner* by Ralph Connor (1909).

Policeman's racoon coat, c. 1890s. Archives of Manitoba, N20711.

FRANCIS MARION BEYNON

FRANCIS MARION BEYNON was born May 21, 1884, near Streetsville, Ontario. In 1889 her family moved to Hartney, Manitoba. Francis moved to Winnipeg in 1902 to join her sister, the social activist Lillian (Beynon) Thomas. She became the editor of the "Women's Page" for *The Grain Grower's Guide.* She was a founding member of the Political Equality League and took part in the Canadian Press Club's Parliament of Women at the Walker Theatre in 1914. Because of her pacifist views, she was forced to resign from the *Free Press* and she fled to New York in 1917. Her only novel, *Aleta Dey* (1919), was written from exile in New York and published in Britain.

TWO TELEGRAMS

I have no patience with the claim that women pay the biggest price in war. It is a lie. My part was easy compared with McNair's, but it was hard enough.

A ring at the door early in the morning. I started up in bed in a cold sweat—was it a telegram? A telephone call late at night and my heart was in my mouth; called out from a meeting I went white.

A strain such as that slowly wears away one's nervous energy, so that the shock, when it does come, finds one with reduced powers of resistance. And it always comes in the end with the suddenness of a bomb explosion.

It was a windy March day, with a cold grey sky. Dirty ridges of snow on northward-looking lawns glowered up at the dark clouds a defiance of Spring's notice to vacate. The wind, with its subtlety in finding playthings, collected newspapers from the wind alone knows where, and sent them tumbling down the middle of the street or whipped them up and flattened them against a billboard. Then it would go wailing off around the corner, only to come tearing back between two high buildings with a handful of grit to throw in one's teeth. The rawness of it ate into one's very bones.

It was along about three o'clock in the afternoon that I heard a voice outside my door asking for me. There came a rap.

"Come in," I called out carelessly.

It was a telegraph messenger.

I signed the book, took the yellow envelope and waited until the door had closed upon him.

It was from the military office at Ottawa. Lieut. McNair had been gassed and wounded.

I sat down dumb and stricken.

A thousand times I had read gassed and wounded in the casualty lists, and after the first few months of terrible sensitiveness I had grown callous, so that it did not hurt to read the words.

Now they blazed suddenly into life. They meant a human being, kind and loveable, writhing in mortal agony; they meant a man torn and suffering in a strange land, with a wide ocean rolling between him and the ones who loved him best.

It meant McNair fording the waters of affliction alone—unless—unless—Oh God!—unless he had died.

I rose, put on my hat and went into the drear March day to find Colin.

* * * *

Three days passed in a vain effort to learn further details. I cannot tell what I suffered during those days. Hour after hour the rising fever of misery grew, until, proving in excess its own anaesthetic, it brought on numbness; then followed an hour or two of comparative peace while the exhausted nerves gathered fresh energy for protest, and again another long stretch of misery more wearing and exhausting than the last. So the three days crawled away. Impotence is the peculiar sting of this particular form of ordeal, combined with uncertainty, which gives the tortured imagination free rein to create its own hell of horror.

For three days and nights I traversed the battlefields of France. I found McNair in No-Man's-Land, with an arm blown off and gasping for breath; I dug him out from beneath a pile of dead bodies, between trenches, saturated with their blood and his own, which dribbled from the stub of his leg. I stumbled upon his half-naked body in the bottom of a trench, slimy with blood and crawling with vermin, and I raised him up to find half of his face was blown away and that he was stone blind.

Recruiting Drive, trenches at Main Street & Water Avenue, 1916. Archives of Manitoba, N2971.

I walked alone at twilight over a deserted battlefield, and as I passed a certain place the evening breeze blew to me the smell of carrion, and I turned and looked and there were three black birds pecking at a long dark thing on the ground.

Those were the lesser horrors that I dreamed—the things it is possible to put into words.

* * * *

The afternoon of the third day there came another telegram. I was standing out in the general office when they brought it to me. I remember groping my way back to my own room. I remember that I stood with the ugly yellow thing in my hand, choking, until it suddenly came to me that the certainty that McNair was dead would be easier to bear than the awful anguish of the past three days.

I opened it.

It was a cablegram from McNair himself saying that he was in hospital with a thigh wound and out of danger.

That is all I remember.

From *Aleta Dey* by Francis Marion Beynon (1919).

73

WILLIAM ERNEST INGERSOLL

Daisy had run away from her home on the farm outside Toddburn village with this young store clerk, Beatty, who now sat holding her hand in the moonlight "flyer" of the M.& N. Beatty, who came originally from the city, was a bad young rascal; and Daisy—who, neglected and exposed to temptation since her earliest girlhood, had developed an innate awareness of "fellows"—knew it. None of her several reasons for this escapade had been the usual one—love. It suited her, however, to let Beatty think that she had come prepared to follow him to the world's end—a lengthy journey, upon which the railway ticket Beatty had bought for her was only good for the first two hundred miles.

Daisy was proceeding daringly, easily, without pause or regret, toward whatever lay in store for her along the path she had taken. Her locomotion was that of a thing which is both propelled and drawn. The propulsive force was her hatred of the farm where she had drudged for all the workable years of her seventeen under that plebeian taskmaster, stolid, selfish John Nixon, her stepfather, and the unmaternal mother whose forename, by some perpetuated sarcasm, was Lovina. The drawing force was Daisy's own eager, vigorous, intrepid spirit of adventure—green maidenhood's hunger for the sensational new.

The car in which the two sat was not a "sleeper," but an ordinary red-upholstered day coach. The two had boarded the train at Oak Lake, the first station east of Toddburn (where neither of them were known by the new station agent) at a little after midnight. They were due to reach the city between six and seven o'clock in the morning.

Even if the car had been a berth coach, and there had been opportunity for retirement, Daisy could not have slept. The hour, the situation, the novelty of the rushing, lamplit train (she had never been on a train before), kept every faculty ablaze and awake in a pleasant

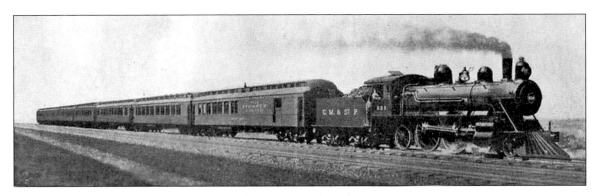

Train flying across the prairies from *Manitoba as I Saw It* (1909).

intoxication of excitement. Elbow on window-sill and chin in palm, the girl sat, glancing now out at the flying moonlit telegraph posts, now about the interior of the dingy branch-line passenger coach. All seemed fairylike to her eyes habituated only to prairie fallow and lea.

Continued

The summer dawn came with the warm melting of the dark and a running out over the skyfloor of spilled light from under the edge of the world. Daisy, her nerves thrilling like the nerves of one drunken with wine, leaned untired on the varnished window-sill; looking, with all her young vitality gathered into shine of eyes and beat of heart, for her first view of the city.

The shadow of the express, as the early sun came up, coursed like a hound along the barrow-pits of the right-of-way, and quivered, as it were, in noiseless impact against the stolid cedar fenceposts that stood still and were whipped by in the guise of staring bumpkins as the smart, swift train hummed on its way.

Daisy saw these effects at the edge of her travel-picture out of the corner of her eye merely. Her attention was concentrated forward—forward, to watch for the first white trimming of roof-tops on the dewy green fabric of the prairie-rim. Hateful to her were the square fields by the track, where phlegmatic men and teams moved up and down the black fallow; hateful the whitewashed houses, the homely poplar-clumps, the stacks of straw. Appurtenances, all, of the life with which she had been surfeited (she thought): reminding her of cows to be milked, of barnyard drudgery, of gawky, red-visaged, wholly unpiquant boys, of men content to smoke and drawl their rare hours of ease.

Hateful! The term is too mild to express the immense energy of the girl's distaste for the life she had, with youth's dash, pushed behind her in one reckless thrust.

She was done with it. For good or for ill, she was done with it all, or thought so, in these kinetic and dancing moments, as new leagues of her unexplored earth uprolled along the endless ribbon of this two-railed track of dreams. New leagues, yes—but, so far, no new scenery. The stations she had passed, and continued to pass, were nothing but an endless chain of Toddburns; the intervening reaches of farm land, no more than linked replicas without number or variation, of the Nixon farm. In spite of the "flyer" and its obvious achievement over distance, Daisy Nixon at moments had the odd sensation that the track was revolving beneath the car-wheels, treadmill-style, and the train merely standing maddeningly still amid the old locale.

Assiniboine Park Pavilion, c. 1930s. Archives of Manitoba, N66.

Continued

It was now about eight o'clock. The streets were filling with the promenaders of evening, each in his or her best "bib and tucker," enjoying the worker's well earned off-hour of spooning or strolling. Motorcycles darted in and out among the sedater and larger vehicles, exploding like machine-guns; in the seat of each a happy youth with either smile or cigarette or both, and often behind him, on a kind of pillion, a girl, with the happily-needful arm placed about him for purposes of support. Sometimes the girl was in a side-car, but then she was generally the motorcyclist's wife. Automobiles glided ahead or by side, down the smooth broad asphalt, like boats on a canal. As the street ribboned away behind Daisy and her driver, there showed gradually more green spaces on the streets. Before long, the houses grew few and drew away, as it were, from the roadside. Green woods scalloped the skyline. The asphalt ended, and they were running on a smooth-graded road, oiled to keep down the dust. There was an interval of quiet bowling along through sunset woodland, with Nature's lawns interspersing; then life, to Daisy's relief, began to bubble and sparkle around them again. They had reached the gate of the park at the same time as two crowded street-cars; and, obeying traffic rules, halted to let the crowd of passengers— many-hued in their summer dresses as though one were looking at them through a prism—dance and chatter and giggle and stalk past, arm-linked or baby-toting or soberly single, until the road was clear. Then the curly-haired young man spun his steering-wheel, describing an easy and rapid turn; and they were sailing down a road straight as a line, with a great white pavilion awaiting them from the top of its smooth-lawned hill. On either side, down the walking paths, came an endless stream of pedestrians, noisy and gay in their evening emancipation, with bare-legged youngsters breaking loose, racing and chasing across the green as Daisy had seen the calves do in spring.

Everybody was "out for a good time." The air was like a tonic; the park like a panorama. Between the capes of shrubbery and across the lawns, and about the thronged pavilion and along the governed paths, the evening breeze floated like a lily-breath, slow and cool and sweet.

Afternoon in the park. Courtesy Mhari Mackintosh.

Continued

The Ware house and grounds were very different from the Harrison house and grounds. No concrete in evidence here—no evidence of money anywhere, except such as was incidentally shown by possession, in the costly residential section of the city, of these great broad grounds, with their natural swell and slope; their big trees, between which here and there a little footpath wandered wild; their plain white street-fence, twinkling afar through the shrubbery. The house was frame, ivied from the ground almost to the chimney-tops (ends of the green runners, as Daisy could see on an adjoining gable, had climbed right up on the shingles), and with verandahs everywhere. It was a villa for people who loved fresh air; whereas the Harrison house, for all its massive and costly ostentation, was no more airy than a prison. The object in the case of the latter was display, the manifestation of the Ware place, good-mannered reserve, with reasonable provision for comfort and health.

The Harrison house was like a striped shirt, a broad-check suit, a scarlet tie, with a blatbump figure housed in them, thumbs in sleeve-hole striding toe-out, gold chain-links dangling, diamond stud flashing, tongue blathering, along the main street. The Ware place was like one quietly-dressed and thoughtful, strolling in grassy lane.

From *Daisy Herself* by William E. Ingersoll (1920).

645 Wellington Crescent from *Stories Houses Tell* (1978).

DOUGLAS DURKIN

If traditions were followed to the letter, Craig Forrester should be painted as a man in shirt sleeves, guiding a plow across a field at the other end of which a blood-red sun sinks in a sky of pale amber. The British emigrant would then recognize him immediately as a Canadian. His sleeves would be rolled above his brown elbows, the legs of his trousers tucked snugly into the tops of boots that reach to the knees. In the distance a group of grain elevators would lift their square forms against an aureole of light borrowed from a westering sun, while a railway train of prodigious length would creep over a gilded prairie carrying with it the highly romantic suggestion that ocean is linked to ocean across the measureless reaches of a vast continent. Or he might take the form of a sturdy figure hewing his way through giant forests, guiding a frail canoe on its perilous course down a treacherous river with walls of granite on either side, battling his way through blinding blizzards with a half dozen pelts slung over his shoulder, or dancing a jig on a log that leaps down the rapids and threatens him with instant destruction at every whirl of the current.

Craig Forrester, as a matter of fact, might have sat for any of the above posters-portraits and done credit to the subject. It was old man Forrester, Craig's father, who had ordained that his son should don a suit of business grey instead of the toggery of romance. Old Forrester had been a railroad contractor in the days when the West was still young and had invested some of his money in a section of land as an earnest of faith in the country's future. At twenty, the year before the Great War broke out, he had been presented with a seat in the Winnipeg Grain Exchange as a gift from his father on the occasion of his graduation from the university.

DOUGLAS LEADER DURKIN was born in Parry Sound, Ontario, in 1888. He moved with his family to Swan River in 1898. He graduated from the University of Manitoba with a BA and taught at Brandon College and later at the University of Manitoba. He played the piano at silent films shortly after the Great War, and his collection of poems, *The Fighting Men of Canada* (1918), was popular. He moved to New York to teach at Cornell, where he was joined by Martha Ostenso, with whom he lived and collaborated. His best-known novel is *The Magpie* (1923), set in Winnipeg at the time of the General Strike. He and Ostenso moved to Brainerd, Minnesota, and in 1963 to Seattle. Durkin died in 1968.

Grain Exchange, c. 1937. Archives of Manitoba, N9874.

Continued

As westerners reckon time, the house of Gilbert Nason was an old house. It had been one of the first houses built in that section of Winnipeg that lies to the south of the Assiniboine River and west of the point where the river describes a crescent before it joins the historic Red a scant half mile away. Gilbert Nason had been one of the men whose belief in the future of the city was as firm as their belief in God, and ten times more profitable. In fact, while his faith in the Almighty had wavered more than once when he had trouble with Labour Unions, he could not recall an investment in real estate that had failed to vindicate his faith in the good sense and the vision that had prompted him to make it.

Gilbert Nason's house was a monument to those two qualities that were supreme in his personality. It was daily pointed to as the kind of thing that comes to a man who had the good sense and the vision that Gilbert Nason boasted. There was no fence, no wall, not even a hedge along the front of the plot of ground on which the house stood.

A wide drive made a half circle which was cut in two by small clumps of shrubbery placed rather too precisely on either side of the walk. The house itself was almost majestic with its three full storeys stopped by a roof of red tile and flanked on one side by a small wing composed mostly of windows, and on the other by a stone porch which served as a shelter for visitors entering the house from automobiles. At the back of the house stood a garage for the accommodation of three cars, and beyond, a sloping tree-covered bank that fell away to the river. The windows in the house were all large and Craig had never seen the shades drawn, even at night.

It was if Gilbert Nason wished it to be clearly understood that he had no secrets to keep from the world and disliked any man who had.

Continued

Here was the great funnel through which a billion bushels of grain passed annually from the broad acres of the Canadian prairies on its way to the nations of the world. Here was the nerve centre of a great industry to which hungry men and women of practically every nation in Europe looked to be fed. Here could be felt the nip of early frost in northern Alberta or the shock of a bomb tossed into the streets of Budapest. Once inside the walls of the building, a man became a citizen of the world, he saw from afar the hands of millions uplifted and heard from beyond the seas the ceaseless cry for bread.

It was this aspect of his work that had appealed to Craig Forrester from the first. The "scalper" who was content to gamble on the fluctuations of the market from day to day and the broker who depended for a livelihood on the commissions he drew from "customers" who nursed dreams of "beating the market" and becoming millionaires in a season, were types to whom Craig could never quite reconcile himself. He had gambled somewhat in futures on his own behalf with such marked success that he had made a reputation for being able to "smell" a change in the market and predict its status an hour or a week in advance. But when he gambled it was to satisfy the sporting instinct within him rather than to realize any dreams of sudden wealth. He had seen gamblers come in from the streets with their savings, some of them with money enough to last them for the rest of their lives, and had seen them go out again penniless and disillusioned. Some of them lasted a week, some a year or even more, but it was always the same old story. The game was too much for them and in the end they were beaten and shoved aside. Some day, perhaps, his business would expand until he could number among his clients men of sufficient wealth to make the game not only worth while but sufficiently interesting to justify his taking a part in it. In the meantime, his interest was bound up with the export end of the business and here his imagination found enough play to satisfy him. Craig went from one office to another of the firms with whom he had been dealing during the past month and arrived at the entrance to the trading-room within a few moments of half-past nine. The room was a huge enclosure with great windows along one side flooding the place with light. Beneath the windows a row of telegraph operators sat behind a long desk that ran the full length of the room. On the opposite side stood the telephone booths above which ran a long narrow platform where stood the recorders ready to mark up the fluctuating prices of grain sold on the markets of Chicago, Minneapolis and Duluth. Before the blackboards that covered the walls, the recorders stood, brushes and chalk ready, awaiting the sound of the gong and the first announcement of prices at the opening of the American markets. Above the blackboards was the "clock," an octagonal dial on which was recorded the price of each trade as it occurred on the local market.

Craig went at once to the "pit," an octagonal enclosure in the centre of the floor where the trading was carried on. Fully fifty men were already standing in the pit waiting for the gong to ring as a signal that the day's trading had begun. Others were coming from every direction, trading cards in their hands, telegrams and orders folded and sticking from their pockets. The telegraph keys kept up their incessant chatter, telephone bells rang almost continually, boys blared names through megaphones or darted in and out among the gathering traders with despatches clutched in their hands.

Craig glanced at the clock that hung on the wall beside the dial and mounted the steps of the pit. He took a moment to look over the orders he had been given to execute, then thrust the papers back into his pocket and looked about him at the faces of the men in the pit. On the farther side he saw Charnley crowding toward the centre, his right hand raised, his body poised like a runner set for the start of the race, his eyes darting from one to another of the men beneath him. Not till that moment did Craig remember that he had neglected to give Marion Nason the message with which Charnley had entrusted him.

Suddenly the gong clanged and a deafening chorus broke loose from the throng in the pit. Arms were up, fingers spread, hands clutched and tore madly, men hurled themselves half a dozen at a time upon a trader whose voice barked but once from the very centre of the pit, the red figures flashed upon the dial—the first trade was made! For fifteen minutes, then, the tumult was deafening. The market that had been only recently opened for trades in wheat after a period of government control throughout the war, was running contrary to the expectations of everyone. Losses from drought in the United States and Canada had been serious and the price was jumping at every trade. Already it had passed the two-dollar mark and three-dollar wheat was predicted before the October deliveries were due.

From *The Magpie* by Douglas Durkin (1923).

BUCKLE OF THE WHEAT BELT. A euphemistic name given to Winnipeg because of its preponderating trade, but other cities quite centrally situated on the great Canadian wheat belt also claim the title.

From *Western Canadian Dictionary and Phrasebook* (1913).

43rd Battalion, C.E.F. LEAVE FOR THE FRONT.

ADVANCE FOTOS
341, PORTAGE AV.

43rd Battalion leaves for front. Archives of Manitoba, Edith Rogers Collection, 82.

LAURA GOODMAN SALVERSON

Many changes had taken place along the river front since Borga Lindal's first memorable visit to the town of Winnipeg. The Hudson's Bay mill was no longer sending its smoke into the prairie sky. It had become obsolete, its usefulness ended when the Ogilvie company built their modern plant down on Point Douglas. The old trading fort was also changed. In place of the long, low log buildings was a goodly two-story frame store built a little farther north than had been the first post. Main Street, too, was changed. A team might now travel its entire length through the town and not be in danger of wallowing up to its haunches in adhesive mud. New industries and stores were steadily springing up and the town was spreading north and westward.

In the time when the Hudson's Bay mills gave employment to the poor, among them many Icelanders, there had sprung up a little colony of shacks down on the "Flats," as the low sloping river bank, running from what is now Water Street to the junction point of the two rivers, was called. But when this occupation failed, these families sold their little homes and drifted north toward Alexander and Ross, that street which was later nicknamed "Icelander's Main Street."

Business houses, mostly of the wholesale nature, replaced this poor man's town on the flats and by this time very few, if any Icelanders, were living in that neighborhood. But down on Number Six, situated about warehouse Number Six of the Hudson's Bay Company, and in the location of Water Street to-day, several humble families of various races lived in the miserable shanties and houses straggling down toward the river.

Here, in a dingy two-room hovel, the widow of Tate Hafstein was bravely fighting her battle for existence. Katrine Hafstein was a tall heavy-set woman, strong of body and mind, and resolute of soul. There had been no time to give up to despair when her husband lay dead before

LAURA GOODMAN SALVERSON was born in Winnipeg in 1890. She travelled widely through Canada and the United States with her parents. In 1913, she married George Salverson. Her novel *The Viking Heart* (1923) tells of the immigration of Icelandic settlers to Canada and is set in Gimli and Winnipeg.

her. She knew hardly a word of English. She had not a cent to her name, but her two children must somehow be fed and her husband must not be buried in a Potter's field.

Some foolish one suggested that perhaps Mr. Harstone might help the widow if he knew of her extremity, since her husband had died in his employ. But the widow had turned in fury upon this adviser.

"Had my husband been treated like a human being at this man's shop, had he been paid enough to keep body and soul together without working from sunrise to midnight, he would still be alive. I would rather starve with my two children than ask that man for help."

And indeed such an appeal would have availed her little.

Only those who have faced starvation can understand upon how unbelievably little a human being can exist. The widow somehow kept the life in her body and that of her little ones by the work she got to do at home and managed to send a dollar now and again to the undertaker who had been charitable enough to trust her. Doctor Towne who had attended her husband waived aside his bill until such a time as she could more easily meet it. He was one of those very few who see in their profession a great mission as well as a livelihood and a means of profit.

Continued

Borga Lindal could hardly believe her eyes when she stepped out of the train in the new depot at Winnipeg. Where was the snake-like muddy road? Where were the tumbledown houses? What was all this hustle and bustle and noise? This rattling of swift-moving traffic on hard smooth streets? Winnipeg was not a village—not a town. It was a city! Its streets were reaching out hungrily over incredibly large areas. Its business houses, its banks, its hotels, were everywhere. She was one in an Arabian Night's dream when she fell upon Finna's welcoming bosom.

"Why Mrs. Johnson, can this be Winnipeg?" She stared stupidly at the street cars and the hotel buses. She looked in vain for the little creek

Christmas lights on Portage Avenue. University of Manitoba Archives and Special Collections, Winnipeg Tribune Collection, 18-6475-13.

which had cut through the town near Market Square. Why, there was no sign of any water! In the spot where the awful, marshy pond had been after the great flood in 1880 was no sign of any water! In the spot where the awful, marshy pond had been after the great flood in 1880 was a splendid building.

"Sure, dear," Finna told her as she pointed to it, "that's the city hall."

So it went the whole way toward Finna's home. Mrs. Lindal was amazed and full of questions and Elizabeth was quietly interested.

Continued

The week before Christmas was for Elizabeth one endless whirl of blinding work. Lace and frills at the shop, stitches and tucks at home. For the first time in her life, Elizabeth had some money of her own. This was a great adventure, but stretching it to obtain gifts for each dear one was a struggle to which she was hardly equal. Still, somehow the miracle was performed. A dollar is sometimes, if rightly coaxed, quite a tractable ally. And so she went one frosty night very tired, but very happy, loaded with little white parcels to the post office.

Tomi went with her, and to see them sauntering, laughing and merry, through Central Square, one would not have suspected how tired had been the little fingers at their loving task, how thin her rubberless shoes nor how inadequate her happy old coat. Perhaps a generous God smiles in understanding upon his foolish ones, and this may keep their prodigal blood from freezing.

There was once a woman with a jar of precious ointment rebuked by the prudent for her extravagance. Perhaps each gift causing self-denial, however trivial it may be, is not without significance. . . . The feet of God must even be very weary!

At any rate this night was one of mildness and beauty. The city was dressed in its smartest garb. It billowed in hoarfrost. It glowed softly golden behind this white sheen. The darkness was an opaque canvas against which the soul of Winnipeg stood out a lovely and radiant thing. There was no wind and the voices of the hurrying people drifted through the air in broken cadences. Now a woman laughed, now a childish treble trembled in the silence like a bird's song and again a deep voice broke through the intermittent quiet like an organ note. And always in due subjection like the hum of a faithful motor, came the sound of distant traffic with the occasional beat of swift, sharp hoofs and the rattle of swerving wheels.

Each pedestrian seemed to have caught some happy vision and so the very air vibrated with an abundance of good will. Even as the trees wore with grace the feathery and incomparable beauty of the hoarfrost, so it seemed that the hurrying multitude wore the fleeting graciousness of a new love for their fellow men—that ever struggling love which breaks forth with such strange ease only at the Christmas season. Against the black shadows the golden lights flickered, misty and soft, through the whiteness of veiling snow; like the twinkle in tear-washed eyes. For the soul of a city is the most wonderful thing in the world. It is fed by knowledge and ambition; it is tempered by adversity and grief; it is beautified by love and honor and it is made eternal through sacrifice and death.

Continued

Then when the time drew near for the battalion to go overseas, Thor wrote that he would like his mother to come to Winnipeg to see the dress parade which was to take place on a certain date that month.

Borga and Finna indulged in a luxurious cry when they met and fell upon each other's bosoms.

"It is not myself can understand it at all—this fighting in a world with plenty for honest folk," Finna burst out in a hoarse voice. "And such dreadful things we see in the papers, God pity us. . . . But it's a fine soldier my Tomi makes, and that's a fact!"

The day of the parade dawned clear and cloudless. It was a typical prairie day, the air clean and sweet, with the whole city looking somehow scoured and brisk in the silver brightness of the autumn sunshine.

Borga and Finna stationed themselves down on the corner of Hargrave and Portage. It was becoming quite a common sight to see the soldiers in that day, but nevertheless a large crowd was gathering to view this battalion which was so soon to follow the many others that had left the gates of the great prairie city.

They were calm enough in outward appearance. An Icelander,

though incurably a sentimentalist, never displays his heart on his sleeve, nor, if humanly possible, shares his sorrow with the outside world. But their hearts were very heavy, very pain-fulled and sore. They had suffered much, those two aged women, and their faith had been mighty. Yet now what terrors did not threaten the labor of their years?

Somewhere a band began playing. It was yet far off, but how clear and distinct the air reached them—sound travels so far on the prairie. Borga was not familiar with these English tunes, but some strange exaltation took possession of her. There was the lure of the siren in that music, there was a peculiar inviting power in the din of the big drum. It beat into the air and the rhythm that followed it became a spirit with beckoning hands. "Come! . . . Come! . . . Come! . . ." That was what it said. She thought she understood now how one might leap over a precipice to follow that command.

There followed a silence when only the passing traffic and the buzz of voices filled the air. Then in loud and noisy blaring the band broke out again. The brown ranks were nearing now, and an occasional cheer burst from the people. But for the most part there was silence except for the band and the marching feet. Winnipeg had given up her first noisy demonstrations. She had settled down to grim duty.

Borga watched with unaccountable fascination the oncoming men. Some long-forgotten pride awoke in her. It was impressive, this sight, and it was part of her somehow, for in the ranks was her son. The centuries are long since the sons of Iceland lived by war. It takes much sometimes to rekindle the old desires. But it is doubtful whether there will not always lie buried in the Icelandic heart a certain dangerous fire—just as the icebound mountains of his country hide, howsoever deep, their deadly flames.

The chill which had benumbed her was, in some strange way, dissipated, and in its stead a fervor which she scarcely understood laid hold of her. The brown ranks were nearing now . . . they were passing . . . they were so fine, so eager, so full of life, those marching men! The two women leaned forward in their anxiety lest they miss something, and in their eagerness to catch, if might be, a glimpse of their own boys.

Finna gave a little strangled cry and clapped a hand over her mouth. She would have felt eternally disgraced to give way to emotion on the public thoroughfare.

"Look! Look! My little Tomi! Isn't he the man for you now!"

Then they saw Thor, splendid in his young manhood, his fine head and proud, his broad shoulders squared as if against whatsoever winds. They followed the swing of his lithe strong body as long as they could . . . and still the boys swept on.

They gazed after them, those two old mothers, and the heavy march of the soldiers' feet beat upon their brains and echoed in their sore hearts.

"Left . . . Right . . . Left . . . Right . . ."

The steady, unhurried rhythm of marching feet . . . the measured and unperturbed heartbeat of the British nation.

"Left . . . Right . . . Left . . . Right . . ."

Careless—strong—powerful! Who should stop it!

Borga gazed after them with ineffable yearning. For the first time in her life she thought of Canada as a dear and precious possession—these soldiers had somehow made it so. . . . They were hers, somehow, these marching men. They might have been an army of ancient Norsemen, so dear they seemed.

From *The Viking Heart* by Laura Goodman Salverson (1923).

Winnipeg recruits c. 1915 outside Marlborough Hotel. Archives of Manitoba, World War I Collection, 93.

Waiting Room, CNR Station, c. 1915. Archives of Manitoba, N10951.

FREDERICK PHILIP GROVE

He left during the first week in January, taking a ticket to Winnipeg, Manitoba, and sending a telegram, as well.

It was a sixteen hours' journey by train, beginning late in the afternoon. All through the trip, not knowing about sleepers, he sat, slightly bent forward, leaning his chin on the crook of his cane, without touching the back rest of the seat.

It was nine o'clock in the morning when, through a driving blizzard, he saw the first scattered houses in the outskirts of the city. He rose and took his valise, moving along the aisle of the day-coach to the door.

There he waited. After an endless time the train slowly ground to a stop; and he climbed down the steps, a little stiffly perhaps, after the fatigue of the night.

On the platform, amidst the crowd of alighting travellers, he stood for a moment looking about forlornly. He put down his grip and felt in his pocket for the little notebook in which he had written out the address of the Ormonds. The notebook was there.

The passengers hurried to a steel-hood roofing a stairway. He followed the stream.

A few minutes later he emerged in a white-tiled underground passage and stopped once more, looking about.

A tall, distinguished-looking lady, clad in furs, swept down upon him.

"There you are, Father!" she said gaily and bent to kiss him.

A lump rose in his throat; he would not have recognized her!

She took his suitcase and, beckoning to a red-capped attendant, handed it to him.

Then she reached for his arm and led him out into the street. At the opposite curb a

FREDERICK PHILIP GROVE was born Felix Paul Greve at Radomno on the Polish-Prussian border in 1879. He studied at Bonn University and developed a strong reputation as a translator and a lesser reputation as a poet and novelist. He was jailed for fraud, then reinvented himself as Frederick Philip Grove and arrived in Manitoba in 1912. His novels of prairie life—in particular, *Settlers of the Marsh* (1925) and *The Fruits of the Earth* (1933)—established him as an important realist writer.

Nanton House, 229 Roslyn Road, 1924. Archives of Manitoba, N15399.

number of cars were parked. She pointed to one of them and signalled the red-capped attendant who ran across and deposited the suitcase in the rear seat, holding the front door open.

"Come," she said as she inserted herself behind the wheel.

John Elliot stumbled in.

She reached over and dropped a coin into the waiting attendant's hand. The door of the sedan slammed shut.

He hardly dared to look about in the quivering vehicle. The engine was running; and with a warning blow of the horn they shot forward into the traffic. He felt as if he were being kidnapped into things unknown and unheard of.

Cars were still new at the time. But the lady by his side shot hers through the congestion of Main Street, dodging this way and that, speeding it up and almost stopping it, as if the task of driving were a mere trifle of the daily routine.

At the corner of Main Street and Grand Pre Avenue they stopped for a moment, awaiting the signal of the traffic policeman. Then they turned the corner and shot ahead again. After a fifteen minutes' run they turned once more, into a quiet, dignified side street this time, with sumptuous houses standing far back from the driveway.

Then with a slight swing into a curved approach to one of the houses, running between snow-covered lawns, they slowed down and stopped.

A slender, well-dressed young man in a huge, grey Ulster came running down wide cement steps and opened the door on the old man's side.

"Hello, Father!" he cried. "I was just waiting to greet you. I am off to school. Where's your baggage?"

He lifted the suitcase over his father's head and sprang up the steps again, opening a wide glass door to the whirling snow.

This young man was Arthur!

John Elliot alighted and stood, bewildered.

"Just go in, Father," Cathleen said. "I must run the car into the garage, or it will freeze up."

Rounding the corner, the car shot away.

"Come in," Arthur said and held the door.

John Elliot climbed the steps.

"Now," Arthur said as soon as he had entered, "make yourself at home. Put your coat there. Cathleen will be back in a moment. You'll want breakfast. I must be off."

And away he ran.

The hall in which John Elliot stood was high and gloomy. So was the dining room to the right, the door of which was open. A thick-napped carpet covered the floor. Pictures in heavy gilt frames were hanging on the walls above the dark wainscoting.

John Elliot felt sobered, repelled. He turned and had a glimpse of the living room opposite—low, deeply upholstered chairs, wide sofas, a huge fireplace—before Cathleen entered.

"Come upstairs, Father," she said. "I'll show you your room." And she took his suitcase and led the way.

Upstairs, he was shown into a small but luxuriously appointed bed-room, with a silk counterpane on the wide, low, mahogany bed.

"Woodrow is away, of course," Cathleen said as if she were overflowing with joy of life. "He is hardly ever at home in daytime. You will find hot and cold water here," she added, fingering taps over a porcelain basin set into the wall. "If there is anything else you need, press this button. And then come down. We'll have breakfast together."

John Elliot, left alone, felt it incumbent upon him to hurry. He undid his suitcase and shook out his black Sunday suit. He washed head, face, and beard, hesitated over the embroidered towels, and dressed.

When he had descended again, he had a glimpse of a young lady in black, with white apron, disappearing through a door in the rear of the dining room.

"Ah," Cathleen said, emerging from the shadows of the hall, "there you are, Father."

She, too, entered the dining room and pressed a button in the wall.

At once the whole room was flooded with the lights of a many-armed lustre hanging down over the table from a beamed ceiling.

"Sit down, Father. Do you care for grapefruit?"

He glanced at the exotic product. "No," he said. "No. Coffee and bread."

She poured his cup. "An egg?" she asked. "A little bacon? No?"

He cleared his throat. "Does your husband own this place?"

"Well," Cathleen said, smiling, "we are buying it."

"Who was that?" he asked, pointing with a nod of his head to the door in the rear of the room.

Cathleen raised her eyebrows. "Oh, the girl, you mean? One of the maids."

"One of them?" he asked sarcastically. "How many have you?"

"Three." Cathleen's face was all smiles. "You mustn't mind these things, Father. I know how you feel. I can't help it. I am borne along on a flood."

From *Our Daily Bread* by Frederick Philip Grove (1928).

DOROTHY LIVESAY

DOROTHY LIVESAY was born in Winnipeg on October 12, 1909. She moved to Toronto in 1920 when her father took a position with the Canadian Press. She published her first book, *Green Pitcher*, in 1929, and she published at least one book for eight consecutive decades. Her early experiences in Winnipeg are chronicled in the story collection *A Winnipeg Childhood* (1973). She died in Victoria, December 29, 1996.

Meanwhile, here in Winnipeg, this was November, the grey season: no snow, not very cold. They had left their own street, their own house—rented now, for the duration—and were stopping at Granny's before moving to a rented apartment. Elizabeth was out playing, in the middle of a grey morning, when suddenly a mill whistle shrieked; then another! and another! until they were all baying like hounds. Neighbours rushed out onto verandahs, then down to the gate as if they could see, up the street, what the whistles were blowing about.

"Why it must be—! The war must be over!" Granny's neighbour burst into tears and ran back into her house. Elizabeth caught the excitement, spurted up the steps and into Granny's door.

"Mummy! Mummy!" Mother was at the telephone in the hall. "Mummy, Daddy's coming home! The war's over!"

"Yes, I heard it, dear." She put the receiver back on the hook. "That's what everybody says, Elizabeth, but it's just a rumour. I've phoned the office and they say it isn't true."

Not true! Elizabeth was crestfallen. Not true, and yet everybody was believing it! She turned and went outside again, to prove it to her own eyes. People were streaming into the street. She followed them a little way towards Main Street and saw that the stores had mysteriously brought forth flags, balloons, whistles and horns. Grown-up men and women grabbed at coloured streamers, laughed and threw confetti. The march began to the City Hall.

Elizabeth ran home this time, certain the war was over. "Gee, Mum, there's going to be a big, big parade! Can't we go? Can't me and Susie go?"

Mother explained that she had different plans. This was the day they had chosen for the family to move to the rooming-house. Elizabeth knew, didn't she, that their own house was leased and all the goods and furniture had been sent on to the new address, in St. James. She told Elizabeth they would be going soon, on a street-car.

"Take a taxi," Granny urged. "You'd be safer in a taxi." So Mother phone and phoned, but she could not get a taxi. "Humph," said Granny. "Commandeered."

"It's ridiculous," said Mother. "The war isn't over!" But Elizabeth had only to go outside and listen, to hear the war being over.

Continued

Finally a street-car stopped. They squeezed on, somebody lifted Susie over his head onto the back platform. And that was as far as they could go, jammed to the outer platform and stuck there, scarcely able to breathe. "Hip-hip hoor-a-ay!" came the hoarse roar of the people. People whom Elizabeth couldn't be a part of, must move with, and yet be separated from.

"You're all foolish," Mother shouted to those around her. "My husband is a war correspondent and the office says there is no official news at all. It's a false rumour. The war is *not* over."

"Boo! Boo! Boo!" shouted the people, as the street-car swayed and rocked. Elizabeth felt dizzy, a sick empty feeling in her stomach. She tried to hide her face in Mother's skirt so people would not notice her; so they wouldn't wonder why she too wasn't a part of this great moving mass of humans, swaying and singing, deliriously happy, chanting those words: "Bring the boys back home!"

At last they had left the roar of the city centre, they were coasting along into the quiet of St. James. Mother pulled a bell and they struggled off the car. Elizabeth felt bruised and bumped and terribly glad to be breathing the fresh November air.

"Are we here now?" asked Elizabeth.

"Yes, this must be the house, 278. Well, thank goodness that's over," Mother said.

Two days later she showed Elizabeth the headlines in the newspaper.

"*Now* we can be glad, see, dear! The war's really over now."

"Is it?" Elizabeth was putting on her rubbers and did not pay much attention.

"Here," said Mother. "Here's a quarter so you can go to the store and buy a flag and horn for Susie."

She went up to the corner, but slowly, because there was no one out in the streets. The quarter felt sticky inside her woollen mitt and it was hard to get it loose when she came to the store. Elizabeth asked for a flag and a horn; but the man didn't have any left.

From *A Winnipeg Childhood* by Dorothy Livesay (1973).

Wood, Vallance Wholesale Co. employees during Armistice celebrations. Archives of Manitoba, N2817.

MARGARET SWEATMAN

MARGARET SWEATMAN was born in Winnipeg on May 13, 1953. She received a BA from the University of Manitoba and an MA from Simon Fraser University. Her first novel, *Fox,* was published in 1991 and tells the story of the Winnipeg General Strike from the point of view of the opponents of the strike. She has also written for the stage.

The party is in Eleanor's back yard. Her father's Men have erected a gallows, no not a gallows at all but an ice slide for toboggans, and they slide all the way onto the Assiniboine River where the Men have shovelled the ice for sliding and for skating. Servants come out with hot chocolate but there's the quick lick of rum in the air, chocolate subterfuge for booze. Wicker chairs have been placed upon a carpet unrolled onto the snow, just an old carpet but the good wool so lovely when it wears bare, and it keeps the ladies' boots dry and their feet are warmed by rocks heated by the bonfire at the centre of the lawn where it slopes upon the riverbank. It gets dark early. Then the lanterns are lit and the servants carry trays of roast beef and sweet fresh bread and pickles and cakes. They hadn't even planned to eat outside, but when the evening proved so warm it seemed natural to request that the table be set where the young people can enjoy the calm winter air.

They get moody, these young folk, sitting close about the fire while the night gets thick and the moon a great egg through the elms. Fine young faces round as biscuits, limpid and nostalgic for who knows what. So it does not strike strangely when Melissa McQueen's glassy voice, chill and pure, cuts

Fashions from *Hudson's Bay Company Autumn and Winter Catalogue 1910/1911.*

the hollow chocolate night with a melancholy song from *Lucia di Lammermoor*. And when it's done, and the silence has been sweetened by Melissa's song, no one applauds, it's like a church. And Melissa McQueen knows, she's won them better.

Continued

> The Unlawful Assembly
> Sunday Afternoon, December 22nd
> Walker Theatre
> F.J. Dixon, M.L.A.
> W. Hoop   R.B. Russell
> Geo. Armstrong S. Blumenberg
> Rev. W. Ivens
> Fight for Liberty!

Like a forest in Autumn, the colours of wood and sunburnt leaves, windy, the pellmell voices of the crowd gabble and crow, men mostly, every seat in the place full, men in the aisles and men in the lobby, with all the clamour of an orchestra tuning, they fill the big room, voices hum and rumble from the front of the stage to the balcony, and above, the restless and baroque ceiling of the Walker Theatre. Russell and Ivens and the others are already on stage, hands in their pockets, talking fast and earnest, and smiles everywhere, Blumenberg telling something funny to Bobby Russell, Russell even cracks a smile, lays his hand on Sam's elbow.

John Queen the Alderman calls the meeting to order and everybody settles down. Up front, a short chubby fellow with a face like a bowl of porridge takes out a notebook, licks his pen. It could've gone sour right then, but nobody takes it seriously, just goodnatured and one guy gets a good laugh when he says in a loud voice he'll correct the spy's spelling when he's done.

Then Bill Hoop takes over, sets fire to the whole bunch of them

with his talk about the war and how the world has become a violent place but it's property that's oppression, the end of property means the end of the labour movement's slavery. Stand up, Mr. Charitinoff, says Bill, stand up. Charitinoff lifts a little out of his chair and Bill says, This is the man the capitalists want to call a criminal. Know why? Stand up Mr. Charitinoff—but Charitinoff doesn't want any more trouble he'd like to sit down he shouldn't even be here with bail posted so high and his wife so terrified of the soldiers.

Now the Government is putting men in jail for circulating literature. They want to keep us at war with the German people, the Austrians, Roumanians, the Czechoslovaks, the Poles. Why should we fight? *We have a glimpse of a world just a little beyond, beautiful, and full of hope.*

Sam Blumenberg gets up, says, *The Tribune* won't name my nationality, he says, well I guess it's entirely unnecessary since my face is the map of Palestine and I sneeze through the mount of Zion.

Sam says he's afraid of criticizing the Canadian Government, he doesn't mind admitting it, he's afraid of going to jail, who wouldn't be? But something's got to change, there's no progress without protest. 1917 was a very good year, for the Capitalists, a golden year. Never before has there been so much money in circulation. And never before so much poverty.

An informal meeting, the speakers most of them standing, climb the podium and stand beside each other, look like vaudeville, look like they'd sing a duet if they knew each other's words and they nearly do. George Armstrong joins Sam, says, During the war Canada's wealth doubled, more than doubled, during the most destructive period in the world's history. Why would the ruling class want it to stop?

Continued

How can she give all her money away? She doesn't have any money, her friend Grace doesn't have any money, her cousin Mary

95

doesn't have any money, it is all their fathers' money and they say they've earned it and maybe they have too. Private property? Take it, she has none. But oh to burn with revolutionary enthusiasm!

Then MacDougal comes to get her, takes her by the hand and she willingly becomes the little girl, led from the noisy house, wrapped in her fur coat, helped into the buggy, and driven into the night by MacDougal. There is another meeting, it's at Market Square, another socialistic meeting, MacDougal tells her, not looking at her, driving the horses quickly down Portage Avenue.

A large crowd has gathered at Market Square. They are quiet, stand around waiting for the speaker, talking to each other, a rumpled bunch of men, labourers and immigrants. She sits in the buggy, withdrawn into herself, watching the crowd. She is frozen with something like embarrassment, the feeling of paralysis that came over her at the Wolseley house, her face hurts from its own immobility. MacDougal ignores her, he's listening in the other direction. Down from Main Street come the lighted torches and men on horseback, uniformed men, and they're shouting all the old slogans, Bolshevikis! Go back to Russia! All of it's been in the *Tribune*. Eleanor hates the repetitive chants, she begins to feel the old dread, her familiar nightmare alight at the back of her mind when she recognizes the soldiers' hatred, Huns! Prussian aliens! The stupid curses, she isn't sure she's awake, there in her wool and fur.

The soldiers ride into the crowd at Market Square and chase the men on foot, men run into alleys and doorways, some of them running silent, and Eleanor feels an entirely new sensation when she recognizes the terror. The uniforms march off toward Smith Street and MacDougal follows, biting his lips, avid as a spectator at a rugby match. He follows the crowd to an office on Smith Street and then there's the breaking of windows and someone sets fire to papers inside, throwing burning papers out the windows, a desk comes sailing out of an upper storey window, horses are dancing and the soldiers sing their chorus, repetitive and raw, Hun, Alien, Bolshevik. And then Jew! Blumenberg! They

want a man named Blumenberg! North. To the dark north end and Samuel Blumenberg's office. The Bolshevik Jew! British justice! And then somewhere, deep in someone's stomach at the fringes of this cavalry, choking laughter.

Even still, MacDougal turns the buggy around as if he's going to follow the hunters on their scourge of the north end, but something in the trotting pace of his team recalls him, something in the gentility of Eleanor's lacy throat breaks the pace, the laughter moves like broken glass to the foreign territory of the north end. And MacDougal turns around again, they ride back down Broadway, back to the river, they cover the bridge with the graceful measure of their trotting horses, down to the Crescent, up the semi-circle of Eleanor's father's drive, returned to the heavy walnut door. Eleanor is so tired she can't look at MacDougal. She is clumsy getting down from the buggy, trails a fur rug into the slush on the drive and throws it, jerky, back onto the seat beside him. MacDougal is watching without compassion, staring at Eleanor's stiff retreat, waiting for the eternity it takes the maid to answer Eleanor's knock. Eleanor standing at her father's doorstep, her shoulders folded around her, yearning for her own disappearance into the house, up to the room, the elegance of her own room the evidence of her own useless stupidity.

Continued

At 11:00 a.m., Shepherd removes his apron and puts on his jacket and bowler hat. In the hatband of the bowler is a white label on which is written OBU. He tips his hat, a modest and formal salute to his employer, opens the front door of the shop, and steps outside. The street is blanched by the sun and there is a faint smell of vanilla in the air. He is followed by several other men, a gentle, almost apologetic exit.

As they walk down Notre Dame to Portage, they are joined by other men and women who walk out of shop doors and factory gates,

June, 1919. Archives of Manitoba, N1954.

trickling out of back alleys to join the stream, a steady increase, everyone walking quietly together, the women's skirts kicking against each other while they walk and talk quietly. Down Portage toward the corner of Main, the wide intersection becoming an arena, filling with people now, they greet each other, embrace, shake hands, many are smiling, but they are serious, this is an occasion for warm greetings, and even laughter, but it is like other first days, when your child has arrived, or the new year, it is a day of celebration and wonder.

Not everyone has voted for this strike. And not everyone who did vote for it feels good about it. But now, it has begun, they have written it on small pieces of paper while they were working. Yes, they said, we'll all go out on May 15th. And here they are and it has begun, this strike, a life of its own.

The crowd fills the intersection and spills onto the connecting street. MacDougal joins them down Portage a ways, arriving late and with a sore foot where his boot has cut his heel. He is limping, so when someone in the crowd calls his name and puts an arm around him to draw him in, he looks like an injured man supported by a friend.

There are rumours afloat like leaves on a river, murmuring fragments blown across these streets. *The Mayor is going to come down. See that fellow over there? He's a spy.* The woman beside MacDougal stands on her toes to see over the heads, to try to guess how many people are here, too many to count, there are thousands here this morning. It is a beautiful day. The air is full of sparrows, there is even a seagull strayed from the water, its voice like an old woman's calling her children back. It feels like summer. MacDougal squeezes the shoulder of his friend and leaves him, he moves through the crowd toward Main. There are no police here, maybe they've walked out too. People greet MacDougal, he sees them smiling, and one man with a child in his arms, the child turning to watch the limping man with the quiet face.

Now a streetcar is slowly making its way through the people. For a moment, MacDougal is walking beside it apace. The streetcar moving so slowly, nearly stops, and the arm of the driver reaches up to the route window to place a sign there, TO BARN, and only then does he look up to see that the sign is straight, his hat falling to the cobblestones and MacDougal stooping, picking up the tweed cap, handing it to the driver of the streetcar and the driver thinking he recognizes MacDougal, mistakes him for Ivens.

Somebody simply gets hungry and goes home for lunch. Gradually the crowd is dispersed. It's a quiet afternoon. No one gets much done today. The man with the child in his arms doesn't fix the front gate like he would if this were a Saturday, or a holiday. There is no name for a day like this. It's the first day, and nobody can say how many days there will be.

From *Fox* by Margaret Sweatman (1991).

Demonstration at City Hall, June 4, 1919. Archives of Manitoba, N12296.

GUY MADDIN

What do I like about *1919?* That he takes a piece of our city's history we all know just a little bit about and details it with completely fabricated factoids that make it the way he wants it to have been. He's just manufacturing a history more interesting than the arid, dull, lower-case one Canadians always give themselves. I think he's trying to right a horrific wrong. Why is it that our histories have always felt inferior to America? Histories can't be broken down into units and compared quantitatively or qualitatively; histories are histories. But for some reason Canadians have always sold our own so poorly to ourselves that we don't even seem to have worthy backgrounds. Which is ridiculous, because our population is small doesn't mean our history is small. It's still full of real human feelings. The fact that we have only one assassination is something we should neither be proud nor ashamed of. But we're meant to be ashamed. So *1919* seems to right that history writer's wrong in one eight-minute swoop. Noam just takes a great moment, with a photographic record, that happened in a period of worldwide upheaval, and proudly insists that Winnipeg deserves a spot as the biggest jewel in the tiara worn by the world in that great year of nineteen hundred and nineteen.

From *Border Crossings: A Magazine of the Arts* 77 (2001).

GUY MADDIN was born in Winnipeg on February 25, 1956. He earned a degree in economics from the University of Winnipeg before turning to filmmaking in his late twenties. Maddin's films have won dozens of awards and some, like *Tales from the Gimli Hospital,* have become cult classics.

Remains of Gypsy woman at Bardal Funeral Parlour. Archives of Manitoba, N1728.

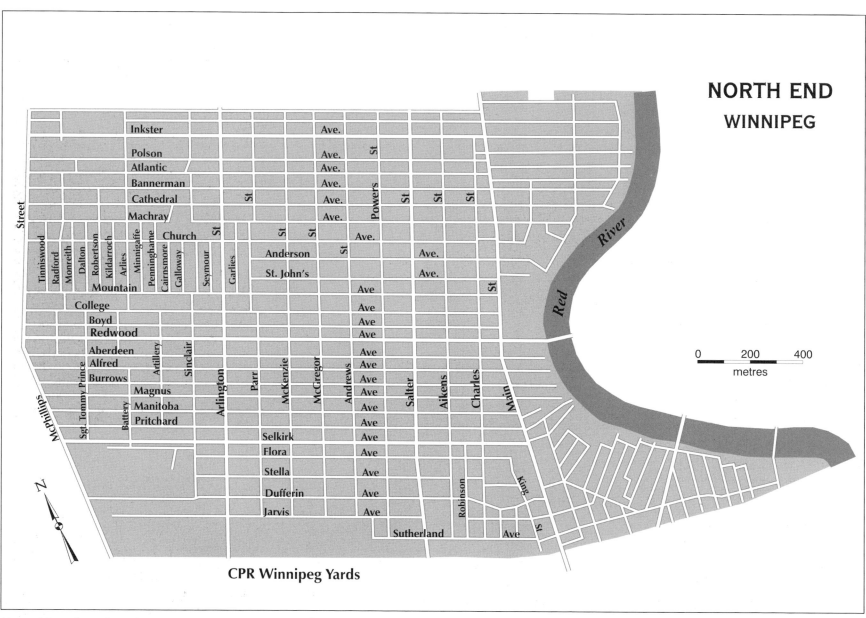

NORTH END

WINNIPEG

Inkster Ave.

Polson Ave.

Atlantic Ave.

Bannerman Ave.

Cathedral Ave.

Machray Ave.

Church

Anderson Ave.

St. John's Ave.

Mountain

College

Boyd

Redwood

Aberdeen

Alfred

Burrows

Magnus

Manitoba

Pritchard

Selkirk Ave

Flora Ave

Stella Ave

Dufferin Ave

Jarvis Ave

Sutherland Ave

Street

Tinniswood

Radford

Monreith

Dalton

Robertson

Kildarroch

Arlies

Minnigaffe

Penninghame

Cairnsmore

Galloway

Seymour St

Garlies

St

St

St

Powers St

St

St

St

St

St

Ave

Ave

Ave

Ave

Ave

Ave

Ave

Ave

Ave

Ave

McPhillips

Sgt. Tommy Prince

Battery

Artillery

Sinclair

Arlington

Parr

McKenzie

McGregor

Andrews

Salter

Aikens

Charles

Main

Robinson

King St

Red River

0 200 400
metres

N

CPR Winnipeg Yards

Above: Map of North End Winnipeg. Previous page: A Winnipeg factory. Archives of Manitoba, Jewish Historical Society Collection, 3281.

ADELE WISEMAN

There certainly was a great deal of vulgarity in the shop, Isaac discovered; more than his father realized. The men and girls in the stuffy factory, which smelled of sweating bodies, were very free and easy together. Not that much was meant, in general. Sometimes Isaac himself thought of something to say that was clever and vulgar. But the vulgarity wasn't limited to the workers. Everybody in the shop knew that the big boss himself had only two joys in life: penny-pinching and fanny-pinching.

There were fights in the shop too, between the workers—sometimes over the work, sometimes over vulgarities that were said too sincerely and taken as insults. One of the girls had thrown a pair of cutting scissors at one of the men halfway across the room, because of something he had said. Luckily the scissors had only caught his scalp lightly, but there had been a big gash and much blood. They had had to call a doctor to treat the girl for hysterics. That was a month ago. Now the two were engaged to be married, and a collection had been taken up among the workers for a wedding present.

The work itself was not what he had expected. It was not as in the old country. There when you learned a trade you learned it all. A tailor was a tailor, from the first snip of the scissors to the last button. Here he couldn't call himself a tailor. If he could have made a pair of pants, a jacket, it would have been something—out of his hands, something whole. But from the first day when he had sat down at the machine, months ago, to the present, he was on pockets. Sometimes, for a variation, it was belt facings—but mostly pockets. Isaac had a fantasy that had occurred to him during those months when the pockets had sped at an increasing tempo from his machine.

Someday I'll stand before God, and He'll say to me, "What can you do to get into heaven?"

ADELE WISEMAN was born in Winnipeg in 1928. She received her BA at the University of Manitoba in 1949. She began a lifelong friendship with Margaret Laurence when they were students. Her novel *The Sacrifice* won a Governor General's Award for fiction in 1956 and is considered a Canadian classic. She died in Toronto in 1992.

And I'll say to Him, "God, I can make You a pair of pockets." And He'll say, "I'm sorry, I'm a working man. I have no time to keep my hands in my pockets."

From *The Sacrifice* by Adele Wiseman (1956).

All summer, my uncle peddled from the open wagon. In the winter he would transfer to an open sled, load Nellie with a magnificent assortment of protective blankets and furpieces, dress himself up in every warm garment he could find, and spend his days creaking along the snowy streets in the flaming cold. Later, he built himself a caboose that was like a little house on runners, with a tiny window in front through which the reins passed, and with a stove inside and a chimney poking out the roof. Below the rear door there was a step-rung where the kids hooked rides. In the summer he sold fruit and vegetables, chickens, and anything else he could find that might be saleable. In the winter he sold mostly frozen fish and frozen chickens. Such was my pride at seeing my cousin Nellie draw my uncle's chariot along the streets and through the market of our city that I have never been able to get used to the alien idea, first heard when I was quite grown up, that peddling was anything but a superior profession practised by a special breed of men.

From *Mosaic: Manitoba Literature, An Issue on Literary Environment—Old Markets, New World* (1970).

David Morosnick's Market Place, 1910. Archives of Manitoba, Jewish Historical Society, 759.

MARGARET LAURENCE

MAIN STREET CAR

till school enforces quietness at nine,
the boys shout (strident, talking big)
playing baseball on the streets,
and short-skirted girls skip rope
on sidewalks where mudpuddles spring up
like wet flowers, from the melted snow.
past drewry's brewery, the car groans to standstill
"Redwood Avenue . . Change for East Kildonan"

(Shopping bag in hand, the woman searches for fare)

Mrs. Riley is leaving the faded house
To fight pitched verbal battle with market gardeners
Over the price of carrots. She reads the magazines, mourns
Her lack of adventure, who for years has militantly rammed
Her floormop in poverty's peaked face.
Her hands are thick and red . . they have washed many workshirts
And bathed many smooth-skinned squirming babies.
When she and Jim were married, they were both eighteen,
She with auburn hair and white body; he six feet tall,

MARGARET LAURENCE was born in Neepawa, Manitoba, on July 18, 1926. Her mother died when she was four years old. Her father remarried, to her aunt Margaret, and she was raised in Neepawa. She attended United College in Winnipeg and worked briefly as a reporter for the *Winnipeg Citizen*. She married Jack Laurence in 1947, and, after a brief stay in England, they moved to Somalia and then to Accra, Ghana. She published several books about her African experience; then, in the period from 1964 to 1974, she published the Manawaka series of novels, of which the best known are *The Stone Angel* (1964) and *The Diviners* (1974). She died on January 5, 1987.

With corded-rope muscles and a job. During the depression, then
Work gone, and four kids to be fed . . holy mother of Jesus!
Those were the days when your belly was flat against your spine!
Now the old man works in the needle trades,
The children are grown, and life is hushed.
Her solid square body in greet [green] cotton dress
Spells weariness, but not defeat.
Mrs. Riley shifts weight from one hip to the other,
And wonders how in god's name the two of them will live
When (soon enough) her man's too worn
To be a profit to the men who hire.

creep along, morning streetcar,
past the shop with the fly-specked window
where the tailor's scissors fashion cloth
with expert snip . . patterns are for fumblers;
he knew cloth long before he knew women.

in the small struggling houses here,
there is a newspaper, gazeska polska, perhaps;
the ukrainian word and the canadian tribune?
or the ukrainian voice and the winnipeg free press.
two voices, two sides of the great ravine.

my city, there is work for many
young printers' apprentices, learning the trade,
where so much is said on both sides,
and in so many tongues.
"Alfred Avenue . . Use both doors, please."

From *Prairie Fire* 20, 2 (1999).

Last run of streetcars in Winnipeg,
September 19, 1955. Archives of
Manitoba, N7588.

JOHN MARLYN

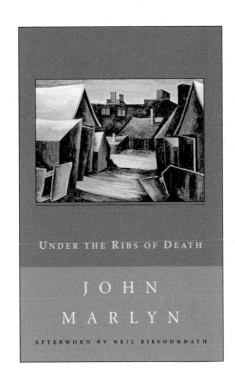

Freshly washed and scrubbed, dressed in a clean blouse and his Sunday pants, Sandor sat impatiently dangling his legs in the Academy Road streetcar. Soon, he thought; and looked imploringly across at the conductor. He had been doing so ever since they had crossed the bridge, and at every glance the conductor had winked and motioned to him to remain seated.

But this time he nodded and pressed the buzzer. Sandor sprang to his feet. The car ground to a stop. He got off, walked a short distance up the street, and suddenly he stood still.

It was as though he had walked into a picture in one of his childhood books, past the painted margin to a land that lay smiling under a friendly spell, where the sun always shone, and the clean-washed tint of sky and child and garden would never fade: where one could walk, but on tip-toe, and look and look but never touch, and never speak to break the enchanted hush.

It grew real. There was the faint murmur of the city far in the background and overhead the whisper of the wind in the trees.

The green here was not as he had ever seen it on leaf or weed, but with the blue of the sky in it, and the air so clear that even the sky looked different here.

In a daze he moved down the street. The boulevards ran wide and spacious to the very doors of the houses. And these houses were like palaces, great and stately, surrounded by their own private parks and gardens.

On every side was something to wonder at. There were wagons and toys lying on the lawns as though no one here had even considered that they might be stolen.

He passed a lawn on which children were playing quietly with long wooden hammers and loops through which they drove wooden balls. He stopped there until a little girl drew the attention of her playmates to his presence.

JOHN MARLYN was born in Hungary on April 2, 1912. He came to Canada as an infant and grew up in Winnipeg. His novel *Under the Ribs of Death* (1957) describes Winnipeg's North End and contrasts it with River Heights. The novel is considered a Canadian classic.

Above right: Contemporary cover of John Marlyn's classic *Under the Ribs of Death*.

As he approached the address which Mr. Crawford had given him, his heart swelled with pride, for it was one of the finest and largest houses on the street, built of solid stone.

He followed the path down the side of the house to the back and there suddenly found a woman sitting on a canvas chair under a tree reading a letter.

Very leisurely she lowered the plump, jewelled hand which held the letter and looked out across the lawn, her gaze sweeping past him to return slowly and settle upon him, in an unexpected, careless way, Sandor thought, an insulting way, subjecting him to a long scrutiny from head to toe and back again several times, but without the flicker of an eyelid or the faintest expression of interest—much as he himself, he felt, might look if he should happen to glance absent-mindedly at a fence post. And yet in spite of this he could not help feeling that there was something in her manner which was appropriate and fitting, something which caused his resentment to fade and filled him again with pride; he was going to work for her, and so in a sense he belonged to her house and some of this splendid high arrogance of hers would be his too. This was the way it should be, he thought. This was how the rich English should act, this was the way they should look, dignified and cool-eyed and distant.

She beckoned, and as he approached her he saw that she was no longer young. Her hair, high and tight-coiled, with a comb like a crown in it, was turning grey, but her face was still smooth and her mouth was as red as a cherry.

"You're the little boy Mr. Crawford sent," she said. "I'm … afraid I've forgotten your name."

He had expected this, or rather had expected that she would ask him how to pronounce it; people he met for the first time nearly always did. But to tell her now was suddenly impossible. She would smile and there would begin again the familiar, terrible ritual of mouthing it, and there would come over him again the feeling that he was exposing something naked and ugly to the world's gaze.

But to lie outright and give her some other name would be stupid. Mr. Crawford would …

Mr. Crawford like most other people made such a mess of Hunyadi that she would not suspect anything if he gave her the name he was trying to get his father to adopt. And it was just as unlikely that Mr. Crawford would notice the difference if she repeated it to him.

"Alex. Alex Humphrey," he said hoarsely.

"Alexander Humphrey," she repeated, and explained briefly what she wanted him to do.

Sandor began to breathe again. It was all right, then.

A few minutes later he was running the mower back and forth across the lawn. It was easy work, clean and deeply satisfying to watch the grass billowing up behind the blades like green waves in the sunlight, to breathe in the smell of it and feel it fresh and cool on his arms and his face. For the first quarter of an hour or so he worked furiously, anxious to impress her with his industry. Then it occurred to him that the sooner he finished, the sooner he would have to leave. And besides, she was not paying him by the hour; she would be far more pleased if he did a good job.

He leaned on the handle of the mower and looked out across the lawn. Two houses away, some older boys and girls were playing the same game he had observed earlier that morning. He looked at them more closely, at the fresh colours of their clothes against the green of the hedges and the lawns. It was as though they were living in a fairy tale, he thought. They played not as he and his friends played, hot and eager and hungry to win, but easily, quietly, without any strain.

A tall girl dressed in white appeared among them carrying a tray which she placed on the table beneath a large coloured umbrella. The children walked over; only the young ones ran. He heard the tinkle of glasses and their laughter.

Something stronger than envy seized him. He hated them. What had they done to deserve all this? Nothing. Nothing at all. They probably didn't even appreciate it. While he, if he were ever to live on a street like this, would have to fight and push and work all his life—the way Mr. Nagy was doing.

He returned to work. But he would do it, he thought. The day would come. The things he had seen this morning would some day be his.

From *Under the Ribs of Death* by John Marlyn (1957).

Interior view of the home of Augustus Meredith Nanton. Archives of Manitoba, N15402.

JACK LUDWIG

JACK LUDWIG was born in Winnipeg on August 30, 1922. He received a BA from the University of Manitoba and his PhD from UCLA. In 1961 he began to teach at the State University of New York, Stoneybrook. His novels include *Confusions* (1963) and *Above Ground* (1968). His short story "Bibbul" is a classic description of Winnipeg's North End.

Out of compassion, out of loyalty to this wreck of a horse, Bibul let his wagon go to ruin: wood could be camouflaged with paint or varnish but where was covering to hide or revive sad old mortal Malkeh?

One day I came to school early, and saw her.

She was the horse of the "Dying Gaul." On Bibul's "island" Malkeh suffered no invidious comparisons, but on a main thoroughfare like St. John's High's Salter Street, Malkeh was exposed to the cruelty of horse hierarchy, and her submarginal subproletariat hide was bared. High-stepping, glossy-flanked, curried and combed T. Eaton Company horses, middle-class cousins of aristocratic thoroughbreds seen only on race tracks, veered their rumps sharply as they passed, hooves steel-ringing, traces white as snow. Their tails were prinked out with red ribbon, their wagons chariots sparkling in red, white, gold against blue-blackness that could mean only good taste. These bourgeois horses had the true bourgeois comforts—warm blankets, stables with hay wall to wall, feed bags that offered privacy and nourishment. Their drivers looked like sea captains—neat contrasts to a slop like Bibul. And their commercial feed was gastronomical compared with the bad lettuce, wilted carrot tops, shrivelled beets, Bibul shoved at Malkeh in a ripped old postman's pouch.

Malkeh took their snubs without flinching. It was part of the class struggle. What hurt was the heavy, powerful working-class Percherons and their stinking garbage scows when they avoided kinship with Malkeh, acting like a guest at a high-toned party ignoring a waiter who's a close relative.

Pity old Malkeh's vengeful heart; the only pleasure she got from her enforced station on Salter Street came from knowing flies used her as an aerodrome from which to launch vicious attacks on the elegant department-store horses passing.

I saw her. The principal, too, saw her, slouched with resignation, a "Don't" in a SPCA exhibit, her right foreleg flatteringly fettered by a cracked curling stone to give Malkeh the impression she had the vim and youth to turn runaway horse. Malkeh died a long time ago, but years before she did the principal had her one visit gnomically memorialized and graven in metal; early next morning, where Malkeh had stood, this marker went up: *No Parking at Any Time.*

Bibul never again brought her to school.

Which is not to say that life on the "island" was without its grim side; what accounted for an almost-blind horse wearing blinkers? *Shnorrers!* Those women with bare feet stuck hurriedly into their husbands' outsized felt slippers, their hair uncombed, faces unmade, women in nightgowns at four on a sunshiny afternoon, hands clenching pennies and silver Bibul had to charm away from them with hard-sell and soft-soap. Singly they waited, in concert plotted, en masse moved in on him. Their purpose was simple—*get much, pay little.* To the victor went Bibul's spoiled spoils.

"Giddy ahb, Malgeh," Bibul would holler from his high seat on the wagon, and his cry sounded to a *shnorrer's* ears like a warring clarion.

Into the lists Malkeh dragged the keening wagon, onto the "island" in ruins like a medieval town (Canadian history is short, but our buildings add spice by getting older faster). Foundationless hovels kids might have built out of assorted-sized decks of cards sagged, leaned at crazy-house angles to astound Pisa. Gates tipsy as Malkeh's wagon swung on one hinge from a last lost post; dry, cracking wood fences leaned in surrender toward the ground, begging like old men in sight of a grave to be allowed to fall the rest of the way; windows were tarpaper-patched, like pirates' eyes, ominous as the blackness left in the streets by uninsured fires.

Behind every window or screen opaque with dust, behind every door splintered from kids' kicking waited the *shnorrers,* trying to make Bibul anxious, make him sweat a little, a cinch for persistent hagglers.

"Ebbles, ebbles, den boundz f'a quadder," Bibul shouted.

Crafty with stealth the *shnorrers* didn't bite.

Unflustered, unfooled, Bibul took advantage of the phony war, biting off the only three unspotted cherries in his entire stock while Malkeh dragged the exposed tin rims of the wagon wheels into the frost heaves and back-lane crevices. That cramped stinking back lane was mutually agreeable as a Compleat Battlefield—for Bibul because the solid pall of chicken droppings and horse dung was fine camouflage for the imperfections Time and Decay wrought his produce, for the *shnorrers* because the narrow quarters made tampering with the scale easier, detection harder, filching a hot possibility.

"Whoa beg, whoa der, Malgeh," Bibul ordered, oblivious of the spying women.

There, among rusted bedsprings hung up like huge harps, torn mattresses resembling giant wads of steel wool, in a boneyard of Model Ts Malkeh and the wagon rested. Dogs scooted in darts of nervous yapping, cats hissed down from rust-streaked corrugated rooftops, pigeons wheeled high above Bibul's untroubled head, returning to perch on overhanging eaves like fans anxious to get close to a scene of scuffle.

The *shnorrers* tried to read Bibul's face: the text was that Sphinxlike tic of a blink. Stalling, he made entries into that memo book, peeled an orange, scratched himself with casual but maddening thoroughness.

The *shnorrers'* united front crumbled. A foot slipped out from behind a door. Then a head.

"What you gonna cheat me on t'day, Bibul?" rasped out of an impatient throat.

The war was on! Horseflies, the Depression having made pickings so sparse they dropped their high standards and declared Malkeh a host, left the depressing fare of uncovered garbage cans (each lid long ago commandeered to be target in the minor-league jousts of the *shnorrers'* unknightly kids), and hiding behind the *shnorrers* sneaking up to do Bibul battle, launched assault on old Malkeh's flat weak flanks.

The siege began swiftly, deftly: a red-haired old woman flipped two-cent oranges into the one-cent bins, her other hand pointing up at the sky to make Bibul raise his eyes and predict weather.

Her accomplice brought Bibul back to reality, picking the bargains up before they'd even stopped rolling.

"Boyaboy Bibul, you god good tings in y'usually stinkin' stock. Look here, Mrs. Gilfix, at such oranges."

Bibul's ticlike blink snapped like a camera shutter on their mischief.

"Give over her dem oniges," he reproved them. "*Yoysher,* show a liddle resdraind," and the sad old innocents watched the two-cent numbers fall back into the two-cent bins.

On the other side of the wagon a pair of raspberry hands crushed away at lettuce greens.

"Hom much off f'damaged goods?" the criminal hollered, wiping lettuce juice on her gaping nightgown.

But the red-haired old woman hadn't given up on oranges.

"Black head means black heart, robber," she cried out. "Perls, d'fruit man who has a white head and eight kids and supports two unmarried sisters in Russia, from *him* I get fresher cheaper by two coppers—ha come, ha? Ha come?"

"My oniges are Sundgizd, Blue Gooze," Bibul, a sucker for brand names, came back huffily. "Berls' oniges grow on ebble drees."

One man's quarrel is another woman's smoke screen. The *shnorrers* moved in, squeezing the fruit, poking tapping complaining with shrieks and curses that sent the pigeon-hearted pigeons high off their perches. Like a bucket brigade the ladies passed fruit up and down the length of the wagon, each nose an inspector, those with teeth taking their duties more seriously, tasters whose opinions Bibul could live without.

"*Shnorrers,* dad youz are," he hollered, holding up a nipped apple, a chewed-up orange. "You god no gare vor my brovids?"

"Look how he's independent," mocked the red-haired one, lunging fruitless after a fistful of cherries. "Look how he holds hisself big! His fadder's a doctor, maybe? Or the mayor?"

Bibul was a lone guard defending his fortress from desperate pillagers; ubiquitous as Churchill, many-handed as Shiva, he had to be compassionate as Schweitzer. Though I didn't know what Bibul's dedication to peddling was all about, the *shnorrers* did: Bibul was saving up to become a Rabbi. Bibul immersed himself in the practical pedestrian, material life because of a Great Cause—the Yeshiva in New York, eventual immersion in a spiritual life dedicated to comfort suffering mankind.

From *Requiem for Bibul* by Jack Ludwig (1971).

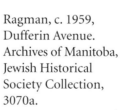

Ragman, c. 1959, Dufferin Avenue. Archives of Manitoba, Jewish Historical Society Collection, 3070a.

112

FREDELLE BRUSER MAYNARD

Why did I feel like crying? I *wanted* to go. Ever since I could remember, Winnipeg had been the golden city. Winnipeg was streetcars and cement sidewalks and stores—big stores, like Eaton's floor after floor of unbelievable bliss. Winnipeg was libraries where you could take out five books at once and never pay anything as long as you returned them on time. Most of all, Winnipeg was belonging. In Birch Hills we were rootless. Winnipeg swept us up into a warm, laughing, weeping, extravagantly gesturing world of relations, all of whom rejoiced in the *naches* we brought them. ("A hundred in spelling!" my grandmother would say, wiping the tears from her eyes. "Oh, what a little head is this!") Whenever, in those days, I heard vaudeville performers tapping out the brisk melodies of "Golden Slippers"—"Oh, dem golden slippers To walk dem golden streets!"—I thought of Winnipeg. There, at last, my talents would be recognized. Writer? Singer? Musician? I wasn't sure. Anyway, I would *be* somebody. It was even possible that I might be discovered by a talent scout and carried off to Hollywood where, with my gift for elocution and my long black curls, I would replace the simpering heroine of the *Our Gang* comedies.

The train was fun at first. We opened the lunch basket right away, though it wasn't nearly suppertime, gorging ourselves on rich golden-tasting egg sandwiches and cold chicken washed down with gulps of thermos milk. I raced up and down the aisles testing my balance. I explored the wonders of the little bathroom—a real flush—peering into the steel toilet bowl and speculating about the ultimate destination of its contents. The trap opened; the track flashed past. No wonder the sign said, "Passengers will please refrain From using toilets on the train While the train is standing in the sta-tion." Just like a song, that sign. I hummed it softly to myself as I skipped back to our seat, hoping Mama wouldn't notice that my dress pocket was bulky where

FREDELLE BRUSER MAYNARD was born in Foam Lake, Saskatchewan, in 1922. She was raised in rural Manitoba until her family moved to Winnipeg when she was nine years old. She earned a BA in English from the University of Manitoba in 1943, an MA from the University of Toronto in 1944, and a PhD from Harvard in 1947. She wrote and broadcast extensively on childcare, but her best-known works are the memoir *Raisins and Almonds* (1972) and its sequel, *The Tree of Life* (1988). She died October 3, 1989.

I'd hidden the bars of free soap. After a while I got tired of running for cups of ice water, so cold it made my teeth ache. "Where are the little bedrooms?" I asked. "Can I have an upper berth?"

Papa looked gray. "I'll get for you a pillow," Mama said quickly. "See, and your coat over your feet, like so?" There was to be no climbing the ladder then, no porters drawing the thick curtain and saying, "Breakfast at eight, miss," the way they did in books. I supposed it was because of the Depression. I hadn't the faintest idea what the Depression was—something about wheat and stocks and money—but I knew it was a bad thing. Still, we were moving to Winnipeg because of the Depression; sometimes a bad thing made a good thing.... And there was a song about "Prosperity is just around the corner"—or was it "Happy days are here again?" I pulled my coat up under my chin, breathing in the nice sweetish-damp smell of the wolf collar, and slept.

The CPR station was noisier than I remembered, and more confusing. There seemed to be miles of track, criss-crossing like the lines on the snakes and ladders board, with freight cars shunting back and forth. In the yellow-brown light of the domed terminal, we huddled beside our bags. Groups of animated strangers embraced joyfully or clung to each other outside the heavy gates. Negro porters—Papa called them darkies—rushed past. In their stiff blue uniforms and round caps, they looked surprisingly like the blackface comedians who had provided, until now, my chief images of the African world. Nobody said, "Hello, Freidele." I stamped my feet, numb in the drafty station, and blew on my mittens. "Soon," Mama said. "They come very soon. It's hard for Mendel. With his rheumatism he don't move fast."

Until Papa got settled in a new store, we were to stay with Fayge and Mendel. I understood the reasons for this bleak arrangement: Baba and Zayde, my grandparents, were not strong: Aunt Lucy was a bride with a tiny apartment. Fayge and Mendel, on the other hand, had plenty of room and no children. They occupied the most spotless house I had ever known. There every gleaming table featured a starched doily, every doily a cut-glass bowl or vase in which dried everlasting flowers curled brittle petals against Time. Kitchen and bathroom alike gave off harsh industrial odors, the smell of severity and soap. Mendel ignored us, Fayge undertook to set our lives in order. "I told you so many times. . . ." The familiar phrase formed on her lips as she hurried towards us. She had told us my father would never make a living in the country. She told us a Jew belonged with his own people. She had told us the children would grow up like wild ones, with hardly a word of Yiddish. As we jounced along on the streetcar, clutching our suitcases and shopping bags, our throats thick with train dust, she poured over us an avalanche of good advice. For supper there was helzel, chicken skin stuffed with greasy crumbs, and a peculiarly dreadful jelly made from chicken feet soaked in brine. I rose from the table, stomach heaving, flung myself on my bed—and slid. Cousin Fayge had given me a rubber sheet.

Winnipeg in 1931 was not the golden city. It was, in effect, several homogeneous cities grouped around the main arteries of Portage Avenue and Main Street. Portage was brisk, busy, modern, a wide avenue with central boulevards down which the streetcars clanged. Its heart was Eaton's, an imposing building of that dark-red brick which has ever since seemed to me the color of commerce. Across from Eaton's glittered the Metropolitan and the Capital, posh movie theatres whose flashing signs, in the pre-neon era, stirred me like the vision of a diamond chain shaken against black velvet skies. Several blocks west, on a wind-whipped corner, stood the Hudson's Bay Store, aristocratically white and serene, with an atmosphere glacial as its name. The Bay marked an end to the business district. Above it, in one direction, Portage dropped away to a trail of shabby booksellers and used car dealers; in the other, swinging around the open Mall, lay the new auditorium where stuffed buffalo guarded exhibits of Indian artefacts and, every spring, fiddles and young voices sang out in the annual music

Kusiel Perlman and his family in his store on Sinclair Street. Archives of Manitoba, Jewish Historical Society, 3174.

festival. Still further along the Mall and south of Portage stood the nobly proportioned Parliament Buildings, one of the city's few grandeurs, with a statue of the Golden Boy poised above its great dome and lawns sweeping down to the university buildings on one side, the Assiniboine River on the other. Winnipeg, our history texts assured us, was the gateway to the West; the Osborne Bridge over the Assiniboine constituted the gateway to Winnipeg's exclusive South End and the mansions of Wellington Crescent.

The South End was white Anglo-Saxon Protestant; the North End was swarthy, European, Hebrew or Greek and Russian Orthodox. To reach the North End you travelled along Main Street (main only in the days of old Winnipeg) past an untidy clutter of Jewish pawn brokering establishments, Ukrainian bookstores, Polish communal associations, and Russian herbariums. Here were the cheap movie houses (ten cents for a double feature, free dishes on dish night), the wholesalers, the seedy furniture stores featuring waterfall bedroom sets and multilingual signs (We speak German, Yiddish, Polish … whatever you speak.) In every doorway, in those days, lounged gypsy women with dirty head kerchiefs and brilliant black eyes. "Your fortune, lady? Read your palm?" They came like locusts or dust storms, like an act of God. One year they smoldered all up and down Main Street, the next year they vanished and I never saw a gypsy again. The boundary of the business district here was the Royal Alexandra Hotel, a poor relation of the Fort Garry to the south. (The relationship between the two hotels was roughly that of Eaton's to the Bay, North End to South, immigrant to Old Settler.) Beyond the Royal Alex, appropriately under a gloomy railroad bridge, Main Street deteriorated steadily past the slums of Higgins and Jarvis to a land of corned beef and rye bread, the lively steaming ghetto of Winnipeg Jews.

There were other inner cities too in 1931: a new France in St. Boniface, built around hospital and cathedral; Elmwood; remote Kildonan; Fort Rouge, Riel's old territory. But of course I had always assumed we would live in the North End, with *unzere*, our people. What a shock, then, to find that Papa's new store was in alien territory, south but not stylish south. Sherbrooke was an urban prairie, street after dismal street of low, rackety wooden houses, not a theatre or a department store in sight. The names over doorbells were Scottish and Scandinavian; we would once again be singular in our Jewishness. As for our new city business—it didn't seem like a real store at all. Papa had bought—how diminishing—a neighborhood candy store.

From Raisins and Almonds by Fredelle Bruser Maynard (1964).

MIRIAM WADDINGTON

MIRIAM WADDINGTON was born on December 23, 1917, in Winnipeg. She did a BA in English at the University of Toronto in 1939 and an MA in social work at the University of Pennsylvania. She lived in Montreal for many years, working as a social worker and writing. She was briefly associated with the *Preview* group of writers. She taught English at York University from 1964 to 1983. She died on March 3, 2004, in Vancouver at the age of eighty-six. In 2004, an excerpt from one of her poems was included on the new Bank of Canada $100 note.

THE NINETEEN THIRTIES ARE OVER

The nineteen thirties
are over; we survived
the depression, the Sacco-
Vanzetti of childhood
saw Tom Mooney smiling
at us from photographs,
put a rose on the grave
of Eugene Debs, listened
to our father's stories
of the Winnipeg strike and
joined the study groups
of the OBU always keeping
  one eye on the revolution.

Later we played records
with thorn needles, Josh
White's *Talking Union* and
Prokofief's *Lieutenant Kije,*
shuddered at the sound of

bells and all those wolves
whirling past us in snow
on the corner of Portage
and Main, but in my mind
summer never ended on the
shores of Gimli where we
looked across to an Icelandic
paradise we could never see
the other side of; and I
dreamed of Meacico and shining
birds who beckoned to me
from the gold-braided lianas
of my own wonder.

These days I step out
from the frame of my wind-
battered house into Toronto
city; somewhere I still
celebrate sunlight, touch
the rose on the grave of
Eugene Debs but I walk
carefully in this land

of sooty snow; I pass the
rich houses and double
garages and I am not really
this middle-aged professor
but someone from
Winnipeg whose bones ache
with the broken revolutions
of Europe, and even now
I am standing on the heaving
ploughed-up field
of my father's old war.

Provincial
My childhood
was full of people
with Russian accents
who came from
Humble Saskatchewan
or who lived in Regina
and sometimes
visited Winnipeg
to bring regards
from their frozen
snowqueen city.

In those days
all the streetcars in the world
slept in the Elmwood
car-barns and the
Indian moundbuilders
were still wigwammed
across the river

Vladimir Lenin. University of Manitoba Archives
and Special Collections, Winnipeg Tribune
Collection, Lenin, V.I. (2).

with the birds
who sang in the bushes
of St Vital.

Since then I have
visited Paris
Moscow London
and Mexico City
I saw golden roofs
onion domes and the
most marvellous
canals, I saw people
sunning themselves
in Luxembourg Gardens
and on a London parkbench
I sat beside a man
who wore navy blue socks
and navy blue shoes
to match.
All kinds of miracles:
but I would not trade
any of them for the
empty spaces, the
snowblurred geography
of my childhood.

From *Driving Home: Poems New and Selected*
by Miriam Waddington (1972).

LARRY ZOLF

ZOLF: ... But what I learned as a method of survival quickly was a concept of Mafia loyalty. You would make alliances with a group of friends and invariably in this collection of friends there'd be somebody who'd be—well, just like the Dead End kids, they always had this bruiser, who was a big dumb guy, and then there was Leo Gorcey who was the smart guy, sort of the speechwriter for the outfit—that's what I was. And I would either egg people on, or have little rhymes or poems on the opposite side, and usually, invariably, the best friend of the dummy. Then I would have this whole gang, you see. And anyone ever laid a finger on me was pummelled by the dummy in return. So there was a price to beating up Zolf. There was a chance of getting beaten up in return.

FINKLEMAN: Where's the dummy today?

ZOLF: I think he's a mechanical engineer somewhere in Vancouver, as a matter of fact. He wasn't as dumb, I guess, as I imagined. He was slower than the rest of us. Everybody was bright, by the way, in Winnipeg. Everybody. I try to explain that to people in Toronto where the challenges in the environment are less stimulating than they are in Winnipeg. I have really never ever met a complete dummy in a sense—even the dummy was a good chess player. Everybody was skilled at something. You had to be good at something or else you had no place. No one would have any respect for you.

No, I find a slum environment not particularly illuminating or exciting. What it taught me, quite frankly, was a double standard. The hypocrisy and the way do-gooders would come around. I can remember somebody coming from Oxford Street—even the streets were interesting. All of the slum areas were always named after some guy, some famous personality, like

Mr. Logan or Lieutenant-Governor Aikins, or named after Manitoba or something, while streets in the South End of Winnipeg were Oak and Maple. There were trees, in other words, over there, for one thing. What Winnipeg, or that area, caused in me is a kind of distrust of authority. And I wasn't raised on Dr. Spock—I was raised on Mrs. Mankiewicz or whatever.

FINKLEMAN: Let's get past your primary grade years up to grade six.

ZOLF: I went to the Isaac Loeb Peretz Folk School until the end of grade seven, and I ended a brilliant career at the Isaac Loeb Peretz Folk School.

FINKLEMAN: How were you—a good student?

ZOLF: At the Isaac Loeb Peretz Folk School? I was the apple of the Jewish wunderkind. People would stop me on the street, old gentlemen with beards, and pinch me on the cheek and say, "Ah, they're killing us, over there in Europe … but a boy like you will redeem and save the Jewish people." I used to identify, for example, when missionaries would secretly mail in brown envelopes the story of Christianity to us Jewish people and try to persuade us to give up our wicked ways, I would read the stuff and I would always identify with the Christ child, you know, walking into the Temple, telling the old fools, "What the hell, what's going on?" chasing out money-lenders, being surrounded by old rabbis who took notes about everything he said. But that's really on the level. He was a Jewish wunderkind for his day, and I was in Winnipeg.

From *Speaking of Winnipeg* (1974).

Peretz School graduates, 1947. Archives of Manitoba, Jewish Historical Society, 3143.

MAARA HAAS

MAARA HAAS was born in 1920. She lived in Winnipeg's North End and wrote about the Ukrainian experience. She published poetry, including *Viewpoint*, Ryerson Chapbook number 150, and fiction. Her best-known works are the collections *The Street Where I Live* (1976) and *Why Isn't Everybody Dancing* (1986). Many of her stories were first read on CBC Radio.

The Army camps.

Dong's blood, curses the Ancient Grandfather,
tipping sideways in his chair.

Half-blind and half-deaf, the Ancient
Grandfather sleeps or dozes in a half-sleep
throughout the meetings.

He's tipping again, says Igor Kapusta.
Golombioski, move your chair closer in on your
side, and we'll prop him up between us.

Kapusta leans down and talks into the Ancient
Grandfather's ear:
For God's sake, Slovoda, try not to snore.
You know how upset Brains Slawchuk gets when
you interrupt the guest speaker with your snoring.

Brains Slawchuk, Chairman-President of the
F.F.U.I., the Free Fraternity of Ukrainian
Intelligensia, an honorary group of five members,
is in his glory making the opening speech:

Esteemed guest speaker dignitary
Mr. Honorable Percival Pshawkraw.
I would like for you to meet the members who
come this evening to honor your presence.

From left to right,
The cultural cream of our community:

Ancient Grandfather Hetman Slovoda, archivist,
linguist from the Free Academy of Obsolete
Languages, now on C.P.R. pension,

Professor Yakim Golombioski, graduate
Gymnast, the University of Chernowitz and first-
class bricklayer,

Igor Kapusta, world famous Bandursit, composer,
Musician, ditchdigger,

And last but not least, Wasyl Skrypnyk, graduate
Come Laddie from the University of Kiev,
landlord-author of the brilliant thesis on twelfth
century Onomastic Apostasy, a private collection.

Mr. Percival Pshawkraw gives Brains Slawchuk
his intimate No.1 smile reserved for widows and
babies:
Thank you for the pleasure, B.S.

He's a slick one, says the Ancient Grandfather.
I can tell from his voice, slimy.
What does he look like?

A travelling salesman for ladies' garters, answers
Wasyl Skrypnyk.

Continued

Brains Slawchuk beats his gavel on the table:
Gentlemen of Ukrainian Intelligensia.
Quiet, PLEASE.
Were you brought up in a stable?
His Honor is speaking now.
Speak, your Honor.
The floor is yours.

Legs apart, his Honor faces the audience, his new
patent leather shoes squeaking with importance
as he sways back and forth, the thumb of his right
hand stuck in his vest.

On the lapel of his pinstriped suit is a 1918
veteran's pin and red silk Armistice Day poppy.

Doro Hee Pree ought-els says Pshawkraw.
Ya neni toot teslevi bootee.
Vote Pshawkraw.

The Ancient Grandfather nudges Igor Kapusta:
What's that?
Eh? Eh?
Kapusta.
Translate the French.
Why is he talking French?
There are no Frenchmen here.

Shut up Slovoda, says Golombioski.
Don't you recognize your own language when you
hear it?

A man who tries to speak our language can't be
ALL bad, ventures Kapusta.
Even if he butchers it a little.

Golombioski raises his hand:
I have a question.

Of course, answers Mr. Percival Pshawkraw.
Any questions are welcome.

Golombioski:
My question is:
I don't like what your stinking friend the Mayor
said in the paper:
All the foreigners should be drowned in the Red
River.

Mr. Pshawkraw waves the issue aside:
A gross misprint, I assure you.

Skrypnyk jumps up from his chair.
Skrypnyk:
And I don't like the government man raising the
tax $2 on the property because I fixed the
McDuff's broken front steps.

His Honor Percival Pshawkraw puffs out his
Chest and smiles like a greasy spoon:
Ah, yes, Taxes.
A necessary evil inflicted on the poor and rich
alike.
But those taxes, Mr. Skrypnyk, are to pay for
streetcar tracks and a streetcar to get you to and
from work, so you don't have to ride a bicycle.

Brains Slawchuk pounds the gavel.
His thick neck in the starched white collar, looks
ready to burst:

ORDER. ORDER.
The meeting will come to order.

Please, Mr. Skrypnyk.
Go back to your seat.

Cautiously, Mr. Percival Pshawkraw hides
behind the table and pours himself a glass of
water.

Now, says Brains.
The members of the Free Fraternity of Ukrainian
Intelligensia will render to Mr. Percival
Pshawkraw, the honor of a recitation from
Shevchenko, in Ukrainian, read by ME.

What poem is he going to read this time? Asks
Golombioski.

Katerina, chuckles the Ancient Grandfather.
Only 750 lines long.
Dog's blood.
That'll fix the big baloney bigshot politician.

From *The Street Where I Live* by Maara Haas (1976).

There's more to the story of Baba Podkova than Burtzik the dog, planting corn in your front yard or gallstones in a pickle jar, though all of them have something to do with that fateful night in January of 1930 and the note on the pillow.

The whole of north-end Winnipeg went out in search of Baba Podkova, the old blind collie sniffing for clues— much good that was— you could put a raw steak or a sliver of turnip on his nose, he couldn't tell which was which.

How it turned out goes back to where it really began, starting with the green-roses kerchief and hoity toity Anastasia, Baba Podkova's only child, who married upper-crust River Heights, the army bigshot Colonel General Reginald Fortescue Brown, Esquire.

Baba Podkova was happy enough to live with herself and the dog Burtzik, better company than Mr. Podkova, her cold-storage husband, an egg candler with cold cement feet and the habit of spitting up phlegm in the kitchen sink.

When God in His mercy shortened her husband's miserable life with killing gallstones, she respectfully placed the gallstones on the oak sideboard under the calendar picture of the crucifixion and went on living.

Haggling for sour salt at the Farmers' Main Street market, smoking her garlic sausage in the backyard kiln or weeding between the stalks of corn on the house side facing the sun, there was no mistaking Baba Podkova's knobby head in the green-roses kerchief tied under her chin.

Late into the night Baba and Burtzik sat together, sharing the earphone plugged to the crystal radio set, holding their breath as the creaking door opened and closed on THE SHADOW.

The fly in the butter was Anastasia, who wanted her mother upper-crust and pushing her to change her name, cut off your leg if the shoe doesn't fit.

"You simply have to bend with the times," her daughter scolded. "You know Woyblansky, our garbage man? He changed his name to Webb and what do you think? He's running for mayor. Why do you have to live in this rotten shanty? You could live like a lady in River Heights. Learn to play bridge, meet cultured people. You really should think of buying yourself an English hat instead of wearing that immigrant babushka. You look as if you just got off the boat from Europe. Neighbours are whispering your daughter is neglecting you, leaving you here unprotected, all alone. Suppose a thief, an escaped convict, a strangler even, was on the loose from Stony Mountain?"

What little I learned of the time that Baba Podkova spent in her daughter's house isn't good. The River Heights bylaw stopped her from smoking garlic sausage in the back garage. When she hit the health inspector with the leg of a chair, her son-in-law, Colonel General Reginald Fortescue Brown, Esquire, threatened to drum her out of the district with a bloody show of artillery and the Union Jack in flying colours.

River Heights is different, alright. It's hard to believe that the people out there grow nothing and cut it down till it grows again, but it's not a story that Baba Podkova could invent. Or could she?

From "The Green Roses Kerchief" by Maara Haas,
in *Made in Manitoba: An Anthology of Short Fiction* (1996).

Woman displaying traditional Ukrainian fabric.
University of Manitoba Archives and Special Collections,
Winnipeg Tribune Collection, 18-5711-87.

ED KLEIMAN

For days in the fall of forty-nine, St. John's High had buzzed with rumours about whether or not Torchy Brownstone would be allowed to play in the football game on Friday. Torchy was our first-string quarterback, a two-year veteran with the school, and if we were to have any chance of beating Kelvin—our arch-rivals from River Heights—then the team could not afford to see him sidelined with a knee injury. The injury had been sustained in a practice session last week when a second-string linebacker had gotten carried away with enthusiasm and tackled Torchy just as he was coming around the end on a double reverse. So one of our own players had done what the rest of the league would have been trying to do all through the fall.

What hurt most was that Torchy should be sidelined when we were playing Kelvin. The game itself didn't count for anything. It was an exhibition game, a warm-up before the regular season began. But what did count was that this was a contest between the North and South Ends of the city. And that was no small matter.

The North End consisted mainly of immigrants from Eastern Europe, laboring classes, small foreign-language newspapers, watch-repair shops, a Jewish theatrical company, a Ukrainian dance troupe, small choirs, tap-dancing schools, orchestral groups, chess clubs and more radical political thinkers per square block than Soviet Russia had known before the Revolution. The South End—or River Heights, as it is more fashionably called—was basically what that revolution had been against. The mayor, most of the aldermen, the chairman of the school board and many of the civic employees—not the street sweepers, of course—lived in River Heights.

Actually, when you think about it, they had chosen a curious name for their end of town. If you've ever passed through Winnipeg, you'll realize that it rests on one of the flattest stretches of land in the world. In fact, I read in the school library once that the land falls at the rate of no

ED KLEIMAN was born in Winnipeg in 1932. He grew up in the North End of the city and much of his fiction is set there. He received his MA from the University of Toronto and taught at the University of Manitoba until his retirement. He has published three collections of short stories, including *The Immortals* (1980).

125

more than two feet per mile as it extends northward towards Lake Winnipeg. So the Heights, you see, can't amount to much more than six or eight feet, at the most. But people there like to think of themselves as living on a plateau overlooking the rest of the city, as in a sense they do. For the heights they've attained are built on political and economic foundations that give them a vantage point of something more in the order of six or eight hundred feet.

Another way of distinguishing between the two parts of the city is by looking at the street names. In the North End, you'll find such names as Selkirk Avenue, Euclid Street, Aberdeen, Dufferin—names steeped in history, names which suggest the realm of human endeavor, anguish, accomplishment. But if you look at the street names in River Heights, what you'll find, with few exceptions, are such names as Ash Street, Elm, Oak, Willow. Vast expanses of velvet lawns, well-treed boulevards—the area looks like a garden, a retreat from the toil and anguish everywhere visible in the North End. The two cultures meet downtown, where the South End gentry immediately head for the managerial offices, and the North End rabble file past the company clocks with their time cards. After work countless numbers of expensive cars sweep grandly across the Maryland Bridge back into Eden, while streetcars and buses pass northward beneath the C.P.R. subway into a grim bleak underworld of steel fences, concrete

walls, locked doors, and savage dogs that seem capable of looking in three directions at once.

But at the Osborne Stadium in the fall, the traditional roles can be reversed for an evening. There, on Friday nights, the North End may once more experience the heady hours of triumph it knew during the 1919 Strike, when it seemed the World Revolution might begin right here in Winnipeg. So, you see, the fact that Torchy Brownstone had injured his knee in football practice was of major concern to us all.

From *The Immortals* by Ed Kleiman (1980).

Track meet at Osborne Stadium. Archives of Manitoba, N15609.

VERA LYSENKO

In the throng, she saw the figure of her mother and father and Petey; she saw Vanni with his rosy face and golden freckles; she saw people climbing into their wagons. The mirage was so real that she could discern the features of neighbours, hear voices, the chiming of bells and shouts of "Christ is Born!" Then, having cleared the walk Lilli went within, eyes swollen with tears, to make preparations for Mrs. Green's Christmas cocktail party.

One day Lilli had come into the kitchen all glowing after a walk in a nearby park and described to the cook the flight of wild geese. "Nobody was looking at them except me, Meggie," she exclaimed in a breathless voice. "Wings shining in the morning sun, hundreds of them, in two big V's across the whole sky, calling to each other and waving big wings. . . . People coming and going. . . . This so beautiful thing in the skies, and nobody saw."

The Scottish girl listened with an indulgent smile. "People in the city don't get excited about such things as you do, Lilli," she said as she whipped up a batch of biscuits. "They've forgotten about the land, most of them, though if you go back a bit, you'll find, sure enough, that most of them were farmers once, or were the children and grandchildren of farmers. . . ." She added, with a kindly pat of Lilli's shoulder: "It's good to hear you talk, though, Lilli. Strange, but I've always the feeling of listening to my Gram when you're around. Don't let anyone take what you have from you, it's something beautiful, right enough."

Lilli had looked forward to Christmas, hoping that she might find a Greek Orthodox church where she might attend the Christmas service. On Christmas Day, however, instead of having the day off, Lilli was set to clearing the snow off the walks, as Christmas Eve had been stormy. As she shovelled the huge snowdrifts, piled several feet high in places, Lilli recollected the sacred Christmas dinner when the family returned home from the glorious Christmas service.

VERA LYSENKO was born in Winnipeg in 1910 to Ukrainian-Canadian parents. She received her BA from the University of Manitoba in 1929. She worked in western Canada as a nurse and schoolteacher, and then joined the *Windsor Star* as a journalist. Her novels include *Yellow Boots* (1954) and *Westerly Wild* (1956). She died in 1975.

Petey would be there, round cheeks puffing out as he ate his egg with big gulps, getting the yolk in golden whiskers about his firm little mouth; the baby would be making dimples in his high chair; Masha and Tasha would be sniffling with identical sniffles as they dipped their spoons into the big ceremonial dish of *kutya*.

Lilli heard the church bells ringing from a distance, and paused to listen. People began to hurry past to the Christmas service, brushing the snowflakes off their new hats which seemed incongruously gay in the wintry weather.

From *Yellow Boots* by Vera Lysenko (1954).

Ukrainian theatre troupe. Cast of the production *Hebolxuka*. Archives of Manitoba, N5549.

DAVID WILLIAMSON

Here, at the South-East corner of Winnipeg's Old Market Square, three one-way streets intersect: Albert, Arthur, and Bannatyne. It's getting on for 1:30 in the morning on a Thursday in June. There's been a marvellous downpour of rain, the kind that conjures up images of arks. The storm has passed, leaving a pleasant, refreshed calm. There are puddles everywhere and the cobblestone street is glistening. The sweep of sidewalk that follows the curved ending of Arthur Street where it runs into Bannatyne seems brighter than usual, brighter than what the streetlamps could normally account for. Only one person stands here at the moment—a hotdog vendor who must've set up as soon as the rain stopped.

The building adjacent to this intersection—the one labelled 100 Arthur Street—is a former warehouse that has been cleverly converted into a meeting place for cultural organizations and individual artists; it's called Artspace. It's carrying on the meeting-place tradition of Market Square; for decades, tents, stalls, and tables were brought in by merchants selling meat, poultry, pickerel....

From *Accountable Advances* by David Williamson (1994).

DAVID WILLIAMSON was born in Winnipeg in 1932 and studied at the University of Manitoba. He has taught advertising and creative writing at Red River Community College in Winnipeg. He is Dean of Business and Applied Arts at Red River. His works include *Shandy* (1980) and *The Bad Life* (1975). His play *Anniversary*, written with Carol Shields, was produced in Winnipeg in 1996.

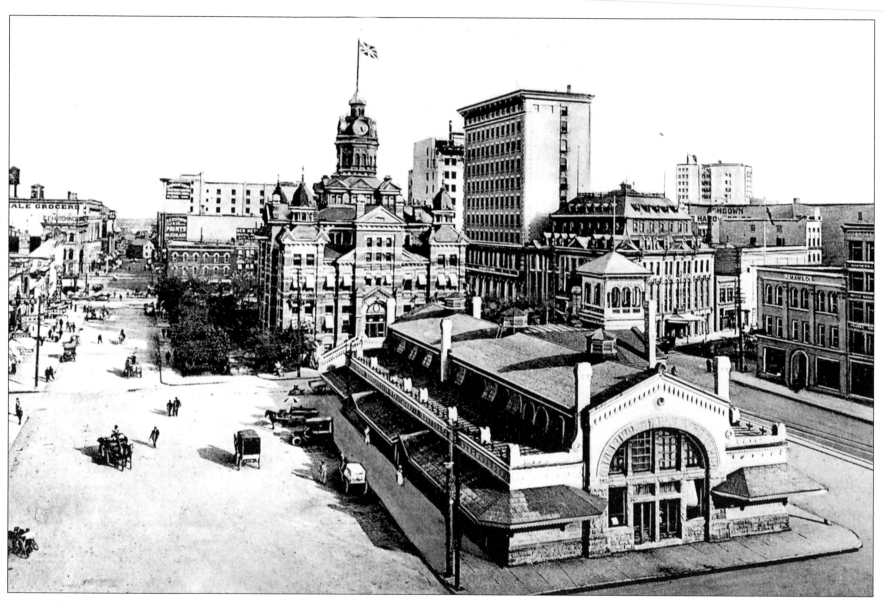

Sketch of Market Square c. 1915. Archives of Manitoba, N8380.

WORLD WAR II AND AFTER

T. EATON Cᴼ LIMITED
WINNIPEG   CANADA
V. E. DAY DECORATIONS

Above: CBC announcer views downtown flooded area from boat, 1950. Archives of Manitoba, N13364. Previous page: Eaton's building decorated for V.E. Day, May 6, 1945.

PATRICK FRIESEN

VALOUR ROAD

listen listen
in a quiet july afternoon 1934
boys playing catch on valour road
only it's not called that yet

do they dream at night?
the squalor and pain
their possible heroism
a bomber flailing through a dark sky

listen to the whispering
unimaginable violence
the brawn of nations gathering
listen to the mutter
of machines
revving in the grove

which of them will join
the maggot cities in france or holland?
whole underground cities
unmapped streets and squares
cities without tongue
where you never go lost

listen to the tremor
along the rails
your ear to the steel
what is in those heavy cars?

the boys perfecting spit balls
the evening so long
and the summer an eternity
on valour road

From *St. Mary at Main* by Patrick Friesen (1998).

PATRICK FRIESEN was born in Steinbach, Manitoba, in 1946. He attended the University of Manitoba, where he earned a BA and a teaching certificate. He taught in Selkirk, Manitoba, then worked for the Department of Education in Winnipeg. He now lives in Vancouver, British Columbia, and teaches creative writing at Kwantlen University College. His best-known work is the long poem *The Shunning* (1980), a study of a rural Mennonite community.

Shells from the varnish ovens receiving final inspection, September 19, 1941. Archives of Manitoba, N17761.

Sergeant Tommy Prince. University of Manitoba Archives and Special Collections, Winnipeg Tribune Collection, 18-10450-010.

JOHN PARR

Early on Saturday morning, Jim found himself downtown, standing directly in front of H.M.C.S. Assiniboia. His Majesty's Canadian Ship Assiniboia, which, strangely enough, was not a ship at all but a large wooden building.

"THE ROYAL CANADIAN NAVY NEEDS MEN!" read a sign just beside the front doorway.

"Well, I guess that lets us out," said Jim, starting to edge away.

"Come on in," said Bob. "Don't you want to make the world safe for democracy?"

"Sure, that's why I think we'd better not join the navy."

Forbes sighed. "Listen, you already promised you were going to come in here with me, so let's go, eh?"

"Just a second," said Jim, bending over to tie up his shoelace, even though it was already tied quite tightly. Now whatever could he have possibly done to deserve this grim fate? He had no interest in joining the Canadian navy and getting himself torpedoed in the North Atlantic. Not that he figured he'd be blown to smithereens or drowned or anything so drastic as that. It was just that he didn't feel like floating around on a lifeboat for week after week after week as he had just seen them doing in that Alfred Hitchcock movie. Why, he'd even be better off going home to Dad. Or would he?

"Look," said Jim, straightening up, "why don't we toss a coin? Heads we go in here, and tails we go over to the American Embassy to see if we can get into the Marines. Just think how nice it'd be lying on the sand on some South Pacific island and getting yourself fanned by a bunch of dames that look like Dorothy Lamour."

"You want to get to know some women, eh?"

"Sure, why not?"

JOHN LLOYD DAVIDSON PARR was born in Chicago in 1928. He moved to Winnipeg with his mother and attended school in Winnipeg. His wife, Joan Parr, was a founder and owner of Queenston House Press. Parr wrote short stories and novels and regularly reviewed films and books for the *Winnipeg Free Press*. His novel *Jim Tweed* (1978) describes growing up in Winnipeg at the time of the Second World War.

"He did? Well, what happened?"
"What do you think happened?"
"You're kidding!"

Jim was truly astounded. The legendary Tallulah Bankhead and some lowly seaman from the Royal Canadian Navy. It hardly seemed possible. Yet this was wartime after all, and passions were running high these days. The young men might never be returning from overseas duty, so you just had to live for the moment. And maybe he himself could live for the moment by joining the navy. He would then have the opportunity to visit those New York canteens, where he could meet people like Tallulah Bankhead. Up to now he had just thought of going to the Hollywood canteens and meeting the movie stars, but what was the matter with going to New York and meeting the stage stars?

"Okay, Bob," said Jim, "let's go in and see these guys."

From *Jim Tweed* by John Parr (1978).

Elks Jazz Band. Archives of Manitoba, N1888.

"Well, they've got women in the navy, you know."

"Is that right?" said Jim glumly.

"And then there's all those leaves you get, so you can go to New York and places like that."

"Oh, yeah?" The subject was finally sounding a bit interesting.

"I got a cousin in the navy," Forbes continued, "and he went to one of those servicemen's canteens in New York. And that's where he met Tallulah Bankhead."

HUGH MACLENNAN

"Ever been in Winnipeg?" he said.

She shook her head.

"Winnipeg could have been one of the cities of the world. Some of the world's best people live there. But of course, we're puritans. So the place is just Winnipeg. God help us . . . why do people hate beauty in this country the way they do? As if I didn't know the answer!"

The waiter ghosted up to the table and silently removed the wreckage of the wine glass, knocked the ashes from the tray onto a plate, then replaced the emptied tray and ghosted back to the door again. Morcy froze until the waiter was gone, then he hunched forward over the table again and spread the cloth smooth, his huge hands moving like a sculptor's on clay.

"Imagine a flat plain," he said. "Not a narrow strip like you have here by the Saint Lawrence, but hundreds of miles of prairie stretching in every direction as far as the eye can see. Imagine it green. Imagine above it a sky so blue your eyes can hardly bear to look at it, and cumulus clouds pure white. Imagine the whole sky seeming to move." He lifted his hands from the table and fixed his eyes on hers to hold them. "Like a great majestic bowl with the earth flat beneath it. Sky the giver, earth the accepter. Male and female...."

She watched him as mesmerized.

"Now," he said, "imagine a building made of grey granite, reinforced with steel smelted out of the best Lake Superior ore. Imagine the building slim and light as a sword in front, and long and light in profile. Imagine it six hundred feet high, towering off that flat plain, with set-backs like decks for gods to walk on and survey the earth. Imagine the sky blue and the white clouds moving past, so close to its pinnacle that you could stare up from the ground and see the slender profile of that building and think it was moving, too. Imagine it"—he jerked the words out one by

HUGH MACLENNAN was born in Glace Bay, Nova Scotia, in 1907. He was educated at Dalhousie University in Halifax and attended Oxford as a Rhodes Scholar. He received his PhD in classical studies at Princeton. He taught in the English department at McGill University. He won five Governor General's Awards during a long career. His work is often nationalistic. His best-known works are *Barometer Rising* (1941) and *Two Solitudes* (1945). He died in 1990.

one—"clean-angled, balanced, slender, light—mercilessly right. And new, by God … like the country that made it."

He stopped suddenly and silence fell between them until he broke it with a wan smile and a tired voice. "Maybe it's just as well not to imagine it. Canadians would never permit such a building to exist."

From *Two Solitudes* by Hugh MacLennan (1945).

Proposed design for the Richardson building by Arthur A. Stoughton. Archives of Manitoba, N7058.

FREDELLE BRUSER MAYNARD

I never once, in high school, had a real date. Sometimes I attended class parties where I ended up making the popcorn or serving punch. But for the most part my social life was limited to all-girl affairs. In groups of three or four, we walked downtown Saturday afternoons and then, clutching bags of toffee or Spanish peanuts, sat through a complete double feature at the Capital. Afterwards, we clustered around a table at Moore's Restaurant and talked about boys. No one in my crowd had a boyfriend. We took turns, Friday night, giving "hen-parties." On those occasions, we waltzed together, slow dances that conjured up visions of happier worlds, and played Monopoly. We also ate a lot. We exchanged jokes, the latest additions to a current cycle. One month the rage would be stories about a cretinous character called Little Alice; the next month Alice was out and the Little Moron was back and exchanging manly jokes. After the first course (we served fruit cocktail, strawberries in a melon basket topped with whipped cream) the whole group piled into cars and drove gaily off to the next house. I had a last glimpse of Celia in the rumble seat between two boys, chin lifted, eyes bright.

Progressive dinner parties were no longer the rage by 1938. That year, the big thing was treasure hunts. As early as April, I heard whispers of graduation parties being arranged. In May, the school put up a Who's-Going-With-Who poster. I hurried past it mornings on my way to class, but after four, when no one was around, I'd study the list. The best girls—and boys—were taken early. Naturally. Some Jewish boys had invited Gentile girls. How unfair. There weren't enough Jewish boys to go around in any event. I wondered if Mama would let me go with a Gentile. By the end of May Sarah and Ruth, my best friends, had been invited. There were still—well, quite a few boys left. I didn't protest when Mama said it was time to start thinking what I would wear. Buying a dress had the quality of a magical act: if I had the gown, I would go to the ball.

We shopped for my first evening dress not at a retail store but at a wholesale garment factory. There was no proper try-on room: I held the gown against my navy serge school tunic, squinting into a narrow mirror while an impatient stock man said things like "A size 12 is definitely too small. You need a 14." I had hoped for a touch of wickedness—Celia had gowns with low-cut sweetheart necklines and ones with a back slit—but Mama chose pink chiffon trimmed with palest blue. "This one, with the puff sleeve jacket," she said, "is your type. So modest."

I had good reason to be modest. Two weeks before the dance, I still hadn't been asked.

From "That Sensual Music" by Fredelle Bruser Maynard
from *Winnipeg Stories*, edited by John Parr (1974).

1950s dance party. University of Manitoba Archives and Special Collections, UPC_SPUB 44, Brown & Gold, 1954.

MARGARET LAURENCE

May 8, 1945, was VE-Day. Germany surrendered; the European war was over. Our celebrations were enthusiastic, naturally, but muted, somehow apprehensive. The war in the Far East went on; American and Australian troops were suffering heavy losses. Still, the war in Europe had ended after six years. Hitler was dead and so was Nazism, or so we imagined. It must have been only those who had lost sons in battle or whole families in the death camps who truly knew that day what the real cost had been.

On August 6, the first atomic bomb was dropped on Hiroshima, and a few days later, on August 9, another on Nagasaki. Harry S. Truman, President of the United States, a nice, kind, family man, took on the responsibility for having those bombs dropped, those bombs that killed men, women, and children in their thousands and thousands, blowing them apart, etching their shadows on stones. We didn't realize the survivors would have to bear such damage within their bodies and their genes, that their children would be born dreadfully deformed, death within their blood and bones. No, we didn't realize at all what the long, long, far-reaching effects of nuclear war would be. None of us could conceive of the buildup of nuclear arms that has been taking place for so many years, at such dreadful hazard to all life on earth.

Yet we did know, somehow, that the world would never be the same again. I was nineteen years old. My life was opening out before me, but when we all went back to college in the fall of that year, we talked about it interminably. There was a sense of terrible insecurity. We had all read T.S. Eliot's lines, "This is the way the world ends / Not with a bang but a whimper." Now we had the feeling that the world might very well end with a bang. We were the first generation in the whole world to know that humankind had the power to destroy itself, all other creatures, and the planet on which we lived. Many of us have struggled against the awful, the unconscionable, nuclear arms race. We have not been prevented from going on, marrying, having our children, doing our life's work. Yet that shadow has, for us, always been there and will always be there.

From *Dance on the Earth* by Margaret Laurence (1989).

Hiroshima after the bomb. Source: www.chinfo.navy.mil.

BIRK SPROXTON

With thousands of others, Mickey passed through the large wooden doors of the station. She passed through as a young child towed by her mother, and as a young woman with her own purposes. I have just now entered the north end where she must have walked, and I have moved through the foyer and past the ranked plastic chairs of the waiting room. I find myself walking gingerly to lessen the sound of my heels echoing in the chamber, I sense myself growing taller. I am glad to have escaped the rain.

The lights in the rotunda glimmer golden across the brass fittings that enclose the mosaic floor. I lift a plastic chair up to the plastic table and lean back. Pinks and soft yellows wash over the curving arches and central circle of the dome. I plan to wait, as train stations require, and make forays through the building as the spirit takes me.

Suddenly I realize that the floor replicates in two dimensions the patterns of the vaulted roof. The central circle of the dome—this building repeats the structure of Grand Central Station—is held up by four large carved columns, and on the floor a mosaic cuts through larger concentric circles and then runs up to the base of the pillars. Huge windows draw light from all four directions and focus it on a central circle. Newly arrived passengers walk up the tunnel and into the rotunda. They blink against the sudden light, they raise their eyes to the dome; a grey-haired man raises a video camera. Another stops to turn, his head tilted. These people seem to salute the dome and its streaming light.

In March of 1933, Mickey Marlowe stepped full into the circle of light, approaching from the huge doors fronting on Broadway. She had walked south down Main Street and the warm sun that day kept her outside until she reached the central doors. Inside, she turned in the light, a full circle, and then she walked toward the arched doorway leading into the ticket and baggage

BIRK SPROXTON was born in Flin Flon, Manitoba, in 1943. He received his BA from United College and his MA and PhD from the University of Manitoba. He taught at the University of Regina and at Red Deer College. His long poem *Head-frame:* (1986) tells the story of Flin Flon. His novel *The Red-Headed Woman with the Black, Black Heart* (1997) is partially set in Winnipeg. In addition, he edited a special issue of *Prairie Fire* on Winnipeg.

area. She did not know that Sir Henry W. Thornton (Knight of the British Empire, Chairman and President of Canadian National Railways since 1922) had died that day. She was on her way north to meet in her honeyish underground cells and to sing her union songs. There was then no bronze plaque to memorialize Sir Henry, two feet by three feet, a plaque erected by the railway employees in his honour. But Mickey would not have noticed such things, for she had her own unions to forge. She hummed to herself, You can't get to heaven on the CNR. She walked into the Baggage Room and sat for a time on the high-backed wooden benches. She made notes in her diary in her rounded looping hand, and then she dropped into the bronze mail slot a letter for Premier Bramble. She had typed it earlier that afternoon. She charged him to investigate the foul treatment received by prisoners at Headingly Gaol. She put questions to him, one after another, as fast as her fingers could carry her across the keyboard. Would he ensure that barbers stop the unclean practice of shaving dozens of prisoners with the same razor, with the same brush and the same water? Would he end the habitual use of the hole to punish political prisoners? Would he demand justice for all prisoners? She said she would write again to arrange a meeting with him.

Then she went into the tunnel to make her way to her waiting train. The shed overhead split the fierce sun into shafts of light, or the rain gushed through the shed roof, or the snow collected along the rails, so she stepped deliberately around the puddles or the lying snow to climb onto the steel passenger coach and sit on hard bench seats, padded with cushions nearly as solid as the wood itself. She made the trip again and again, to Prince Albert, to Saskatoon, to Regina and Moose Jaw. To Flin Flon. And one last time from Dauphin en route to Portage la Prairie Gaol for Women with an entourage of officers, dozens of them smiling and swaggering and among them the clammy clinging smile of a female officer, who stood grinning outside the wooden door of the toilet cubicle.

The rotunda echoes with sounds of the past, the times between Mickey's time and now. Passengers from Europe and the United States on their way to Churchill on the Muskeg Express. They have moved through here laden with cameras and stories of the polar bears they would see in close-up. Glenn Gould travelled through here and his trip on the Muskeg led to his radio program on "The Idea of North," a collage of voices held together by a background track of railroad sounds to form the spine of his narrative. Gould fragmented the voices into bits of sound and inflection: his voices do not speak together in conversation, but rather play against each other, in counterpoint. Gould's "Idea" delivers over to his listener the pleasure of making the story. He leaves it to you to fill in the gaps. Mickey too had an idea of north. (A toddler's hi hi hi echoes and rolls through the dome. A young boy tells the ice cream vendor that the Vancouver train has been delayed.)

From *The Red-Headed Woman with the Black, Black Heart*
by Birk Sproxton (1997).

Union Station. Archives of Manitoba, N10937.

MARSHALL McLUHAN

McLUHAN: Winnipeg is a bi-cultural city. It is bi-lingual and bi-cultural in large degree. The one I grew up in was. And it's a very rich cultural centre.

EASTERBROOK: I think there's some confusion in the question you're raising, though. There seems to be some assumption, you know, that a high rate of growth, of gross national product or population increase is necessarily a good thing. As a place to live, as a place where there is balance and a sense of belonging....

McLUHAN: I lived on Gertrude Avenue and there was the Assiniboine River at one end of the street, a few hundred yards away; at the other end was the Red River. I had a boat on each river, a rowboat on the Assiniboine where I skied in winter and a sailboat on the Red. The opportunities for games and sports out of doors there are absolutely unlimited, and all within walking distance of your own house. The human scale is a very important fact about Winnipeg. Very few cities retain that human scale where the individual still has significant dimension, and a city in which people can actually make their way around without too much strain.

FINKLEMAN: Well, I like Winnipeg very much but all I was saying was that it seems that areas of economic growth seem to attract talented people. That's all I was saying, that unfortunately people are duped into believing that Toronto is a great place to live and so a lot of creative, talented young people leave Winnipeg for Toronto because they're caught up in this whole idea of a boom town.

EASTERBROOK: But a great many talented people stay too.

FINKLEMAN: But I think it could be better. It could be better if the people of Winnipeg could be convinced that it was a terrific place. I think it is.

HERBERT MARSHALL McLUHAN was born in Edmonton in 1911 and moved with his parents to Winnipeg in 1915. He attended the University of Manitoba, where he received a BA (Hons.) in 1933 and an MA in 1934. He received his doctorate from Cambridge in 1943. He taught for most of his life at the University of Toronto. McLuhan became one of the most popular media gurus in the world. His works *The Gutenberg Galaxy* (1962) and *Understanding Media: The Extensions of Man* (1964) had immense influence. He died in 1979.

McLUHAN: There's a sucker born every minute, that's what you're saying, and they'll always take that view, that the big town is the place for me.

FINKLEMAN: So that's one thing you have to tell Winnipeggers, that a town of 500,000 just might be the perfect size—little crime, five minutes from work.

McLUHAN: But notice that the people who make it in the world today can live in small towns. Bucky Fuller and such can live in tiny little towns anywhere in the world. There is no need to live anywhere in particular in the world today in order to be a world figure. You can be a world figure in any little town anywhere.

From *Speaking of Winnipeg* (1974).

Sailing and rowboats. University of Manitoba Archives and Special Collections, Winnipeg Tribune Collection, 18-6292-3.

ROY DANIELLS

FAREWELL TO WINNIPEG

So I remember you, the brightening city
Of snows and summer storms and shining days;
So shall my mind recall you in amazement,
Dazed with the past, its wonder and its pity.

While the clouds mass in storm, turn and repass,
What forms are these that hourly hover over,
Cover the city and again discover
Dim faces while the night winds westward press?

While the skies cloud, repass again and mass,
What forms, what faces, voices in the wind?
Crying from the farthest darkness of my mind
Even as the westward winds cry in the grass.

While the winds rise, while the clouds westward move,
What tumults mourn aloud, what portents form
In storm of memories and murmur of doom
In ireful skies where over the city heave,

ROY DANIELLS was born in 1902 in London, England. His family moved to Victoria, British Columbia, in 1910. He studied at the University of British Columbia and taught at the universities of Toronto, Manitoba, and British Columbia. He published two books of verse, *Deeper into the Forest* (1948) and *The Chequered Shade* (1963).

Hover, form and reform the shock troops
And the armour of the storm. O city unsung,
They ring your triumph; with prophetic tongue
They tell your destiny and imminent doom.

Farewell to Winnipeg, the snow-bright city
Set in the prairie distance without bound
Profound and fathomless, encompassed round
By the wind-haunted country and wide winter.

Farewell to Winnipeg, the sun-bright city
Lapped in light summer leaves by turning waters,
Lost in a level land of endless acres,
Found in the endless memories of my heart.

From *Mosaic: Manitoba in Literature* 3, 3 (1970).

The Nutty Club building in wintertime. Photo by Ben MacPhee-Sigurdson.

CITY OF DREADFUL NIGHT

Above: Row housing. University of Manitoba Archives and Special Collections, Tribune Collection, 18-2814-8. Previous page: Winnipeg underpass, "Warriors for Jesus" sprayed on concrete. University of Manitoba Archives and Special Collections, Tribune Collection, 18-6261-168.

ADELE WISEMAN

It would be unfair to suggest that during the years that followed, Hoda tried to erase all memory of her black night and of the existence of a living issue. True, other pains and other pleasures dulled the intensity of recall; gradually a shadow formed over the area in her memory, a shadow that gained in opacity with time, so that, like the craters of the moon, from a distance the dark spot seemed more like a smudge on an unbroken surface than like the pit into which she knew she could fall if she allowed herself to venture too close. But she could not pretend the smudge wasn't there. What had happened had happened, and Hoda was not capable of forgetting entirely. But she allowed herself to temporize with memory, promising herself, as time passed, that one day, as soon as she had a chance, tomorrow, maybe, or the day after, she would sit down and try to figure out what meaning that distant night and the living souvenir which it was sometimes so difficult to believe really existed, had in her life. She still walked blocks out of her way when the occasion arose, rather than pass anywhere near the Orphanage, which was for her the geographic incarnation of the shadow pit in her mind which she dared not approach too closely. With time, the shadowed area did appear to shrink, for Hoda had many other things to think about. Those few forbidden blocks around the Orphanage also shrank, as Hoda grew more familiar with the wide expanse of the city which existed beyond the bounds which had had meaning for her in childhood. But she could not simply forget, and though she now had a proper contempt for silly, impractical, childish fantasies, Hoda still believed that in the endless folds of time that were yet to unwrinkle before her, were hidden all the correct solutions to all her problems, and she promised herself that she would make good all her errors, the minute the proper shape of her destiny was revealed to her.

Meanwhile she continued to do her best, and became, in time, well enough known for it in the district to have earned for herself a fairly regular flow of clientele and a certain degree of notoriety among decent folk. Of the latter Hoda was to some extent aware, and when it was, occasionally, underlined for her attention, she expressed a large, contemptuous willingness to be tolerant of public opinion if the public would, on its side, keep its opinion to itself, and not bother her and her daddy with it. Among themselves, if people wanted to talk about her, let them. Her touchy spot was, of course, her daddy. For herself Hoda didn't give a damn what any bunch of busybodies thought. What did they know about her life? And what did they care, either, about the important things? But close to the surface of her defiance was always the fear that someday, someone would bludgeon his or her way through her father's innocence. It would take a bludgeon, it seemed to her sometimes, to break its way through that amazingly tough shell of softness, in which the most obvious revelation of the truth lost its shape and disappeared. But someday, nevertheless, it might happen, perhaps in the jigsaw way she used to think babies were put together in the dark. Danile would submit to endless violations in his darkness, but one day a final clue would be left that would, though he struggled against it, force the fullness of knowledge on him, and even to Danile the blind, the ugly truth would be born. Oddly enough it was only in relation to her father that Hoda saw it as an ugly truth. For the rest, as she did not tire of asserting when she discussed it with her friends, she didn't give a damn what they thought; they were all hypocrites anyway.

From *Crackpot* by Adele Wiseman (1974).

Stony Mountain Penitentiary Administration Building. Archives of Manitoba.

FREDERICK PHILIP GROVE

A few miles north of the great city of the plains there rises, abruptly, out of the level prairie, the brow of a hill. It does not look imposing from a distance.

But as, coming from the city, you approach it, driving perhaps in a car, and as the hill rises before you, it is apt to take on, in the impression it makes on your imagination, much larger proportions than its natural dimensions would warrant.

That impression is due to the sinister suggestiveness of the work of man. For the brow of the hill is crowned with a group of buildings of truly Titanic outline.

A perpendicular wall rises up, fifty feet high, many feet thick: a smooth wall, built of limestone blocks, stretching for several hundred feet from east to west, and forming behind a perfect square by its enclosure. In the centre of the south end there is a gate, wide and high, but completely closed by steel bars four inches apart. A man, armed from head to foot, always paces the arched gateway behind.

From *Settlers of the Marsh* by Frederick Philip Grove (1966).

JOHN PETER

conference of architects some years before had unanimously voted the avenue between the campus and the city the most hideous in all Canada.... A demented cat's cradle of wires and cables formed a grid of ugliness above the roadway, which garish billboards to left and right did nothing to relieve, and every grimy shopfront he passed was crowned with a scrawl of unlit neon tubing. Even in summer, with the green of lawns and trees to freshen it, the vista was unappealing; now, with dusty leaves littering the sallow grass, it was squalid, a five-mile gutter of slums and seediness. God, what a place!

[Ed. Note. Here, John Peter casts a bleak eye on Pembina Highway.]

From *Take Hands at Winter* by John Peter (1967).

JOHN PETER was born in South Africa. He studied in England and then taught briefly at the University of Manitoba before moving to British Columbia. His novel *Take Hands at Winter* (1967) is set in an unnamed city that could be no place but Winnipeg. The novel deals with academics who, among other things, despise prairie poetry.

ROBERT HUNTER

The city is dying. A pall of silence seeps from the cracks and fissures. Crowds bundled in overcoats and parkas are milling along the pavement. The cogs and wheels are turning effortlessly, but in the wrong direction. The iced-over concrete is as cheery as a tombstone. The cars are all hearses. Buses are cattle-cars on their way to Buchenwald. There is no heat, no love, no lair—only death and the process of dying. Collapse, agony, horror, claustrophobia, gangrene, bile....

I shuffle instead of walking, because I am too cold and exhausted to walk like a man. The buildings are all grey. Distant figures are grey. The atmosphere is a poisonous green. I'm itching in the middle of my brain, where it's impossible.

Continued

Summer fattens and overflows into every last nook and cranny. The arid prairie wind, with its pollen, moves in from the west. Dust-clouds lie like bruises in the flesh of the horizon. Odours rise from every culvert and gutter. The ventilators begin to pant, shooting fetid gusts of halitosis into alleys and lanes. The slaughterhouse, its raw stink stopped in its tracks by the ice all winter, now blooms like a tree of death, sending whiffs of excrement and rotting organs blowing for miles on the winds. The neighbourhood radiating out around the plant visibly cowers. Flowers wilt. Grass turns yellow. Windows are fogged, as though sprayed with mosquito poison. It is only in the morning, when the dew is still heavy, that the air is palatable. Or during a rain. Otherwise, dense soapy heat-waves ripple across the streets around the slaughterhouse, like fumes dancing across a quagmire or bog. This is what Buchenwald must have looked like in its hey-day. Black crematorium smoke pouring from chimney stacks, fine flecks of ash drifting about like

ROBERT HUNTER was born in St. Boniface, Manitoba, on October 13, 1941. He worked briefly as a reporter for the *Winnipeg Tribune* before moving to Vancouver, where he became a cofounder of Greenpeace, the environmental organization he led until 1977. His novel *Erebus* (1968) is set in Winnipeg. The horror of the stockyards touches every aspect of life in Winnipeg. Robert Hunter passed away on May 2, 2005.

seeds, faint shrieks that prickle the eardrums all day—even miles away. And the clockwork whack, whack, whack of a gun. Meanwhile, the sun cauterizes the streets. The sweat on your feet brings up blisters. The whole city has been turned into a mirage melting slowly into a frying pan.

From *Erebus* by Robert Hunter (1968).

Interior view of stockyard. Archives of Manitoba, N8739.

MORT FORER

Toinette had never before come to the city to become part of it, even for a little while. She had slipped in and out of this concrete forest many, many times before, but always specifically to take something from it—from the salvage stores where she bought the last useful part of whatever was sold, occasionally from the basements of the huge department stores where she picked through the soiled things, altering price tags. And those special times—Hallowe'en times—when she and the kids and the neighbours and the whole Humback, masked and costumed and painted, invaded the city with sacks and boxes and begging chants. But even then she was within the great mob of her own that came together and then left.

All dressed up for Hallowe'en. University of
Manitoba Archives and Special Collections, 18-2663-14.

This time 'Toinette came to the city as an immigrant. . . . Yet she refused to ask directions of anyone. Instinctively she pointed herself east toward the grey river and north toward the black railway tracks. . . .

Three miles through the centre of the city into the off-main-street squalor, she waddled, a dark, self-conscious, semi-enclosed, semi-dwarf . . . short-breathed against the acrid smells, short-stepping within the constant flow around her, pricked in her ears by the sharp heel-clicks on the concrete, the half-words that floated by, the tenor blasts of the buses and the trucks—but beyond all, vaguely conscious of a strange uncertainty of her own reality, as if watching herself watch.

From *The Humback* by Mort Forer (1969).

MORT FORER was born in Brooklyn in 1922. He came to Canada in 1941 to enlist in the Canadian Army, and he served in Europe for four and a half years. He was wounded in action and decorated. He married Winnipeg-born film actress and writer Marion Waldman, who conceived of and wrote the television series *Sussex Street*, and also co-wrote several television and radio pieces with Forer. They lived in Winnipeg from 1950 to 1965. Mort Forer was a social worker in Métis communities in eastern Manitoba, and his best-known work, the novel *The Humback* (1969), deals with those communities. Mort Forer died in 1981 at the age of sixty.

JAMES REANEY

A MESSAGE TO WINNIPEG

ii) Winnipeg Seen as a Body of Time and Space

Winnipeg, what once were you. You were,
Your hair was grass by the river ten feet tall,
Your arms were burr oaks and ash leaf maples,
Your backbone was a crooked silver muddy river,
Your thoughts were ravens in flocks, your bones were
    Snow,
Your legs were trails and your blood was a people
     Who did what the stars did and the sun.

Then what were you? You were cracked enamel like
Into parishes and strips that come down to the river.
Convents were built, the river lined with nuns
Praying and windmills turning and your people
Had a blood that did what a star did and a Son.

JAMES REANEY was born in Stratford, Ontario. He attended the University of Toronto, then taught in the English department of the University of Manitoba for ten years. He edited *Alphabet Magazine,* and two of his volumes of poetry, *The Red Heart* (1949) and *A Suit of Nettles* (1958), won the Governor General's Award for poetry.

Then on top of you fell
A boneyard of wrecked auto gent, his hair
Made of rusted car door handles, his fingernails
Of red Snowflake Pastry signs, his belly
Of buildings downtown; his arms of sewers,
His nerves electric wires, his mouth a telephone,
His backbone—a cracked cement street. His heart
An orange pendulum bus crawling with the human fleas
Of a so-so civilization—half gadget, half flesh—
        I don't know what I would have instead—
        And they did what they did more or less.

From *Selected Shorter Poems* by James Reaney (1975).

Winnipeg area junkyard. University of
Manitoba Archives and Special Collections,
Winnipeg Tribune Collection, 18-514-22.

BEATRICE CULLETON

BEATRICE CULLETON (now Mosionier) was born in Winnipeg in 1949. At the age of three, she became a ward of the Children's Aid Society in Winnipeg and spent most of her youth in foster homes. Her best-known work is the novel *In Search of April Raintree* (1983).

"Oh, I don't know. In this atmosphere everything is staged. It's romanticized. On Monday we'll all go home and to what? I'll go back to see the drunken Indians on Main Street and I'll feel the same old shame. It's like having two worlds in my life that can't be mixed. And I've made my choice on how I want to live my everyday life."

"Yeah, but the Indian blood runs through your veins, April. To deny that, you deny a basic part of yourself. You'll never be satisfied until you can accept that fact."

"How do you do it, Cheryl? How is it that you're so proud when there's so much against being a native person?"

"For one thing, I don't see it that way. Maybe I have put too much faith in my dreams. But if alcohol didn't have such a destructive force on us, we'd be a fabulous people. And that's what I see. I see all the possibilities that we have. Nancy, for instance, you never did think much of her when I was attending university, did you? Well, she does drink and does other things that you would never dream of doing. But she also holds a steady job and she's been at the minimum wage for a long time. They use her and she knows it. And she gets depressed about it. But with her education and the way things are, she knows she doesn't have many choices. She helps support her mother and her sister and a brother. The reason why she left home in the first place was her father. He was an alcoholic who beat her mother up and raped Nancy. Okay, she doesn't have much, maybe she never will have much, but what she's got she shares with her family. And she's not an exception."

"I didn't know that," I said. We sat for a time in silence before I spoke again.

"When we lived with our parents, I used to take you to the park. The white kids would call the native kids all sorts of names. If they had let us, I would have played with the white kids.

Never the native kids. To me, the white kids were the winners all the way. I guess what I feel today started back then. It would take an awful lot for me to be able to change what I've felt for a lifetime. Shame doesn't dissolve overnight."

"I can understand that. Me, I've been identifying with the Indian people ever since I was a kid. The Métis people share more of the same problems with the Indian people. I guess that's why Riel was leader to both. I wrote this one piece in university but they wouldn't publish it because they said it was too controversial. I still know it by heart. Want to hear it?"

"Sure," I said. There was little in our conversation we hadn't discussed before, but sitting there in our tent, surrounded by proud Indians, everything seemed different.

White Man, to you my voice is like the unheard call in the wilderness. It is there, though you do not hear. But this once, take the time to listen to what I have to say.

Your history is highlighted by your wars. Why is it all right for your nations to conquer each other in your attempts at domination? When you sailed to our lands, you came with your advanced weapons. Warfare which could destroy all men, all creation. And you allow such power to be in the hands of those few who have such little value in true wisdom.

White Man, when you first came, most of our tribes began with peace and trust in dealing with you, strange white intruders. We showed you how to survive in our homelands. We were willing to share with you our vast wealth. Instead of repaying us with gratitude, you, White Man, turned on us, your friends. You turned on us with your advanced weapons and your cunning trickery.

When we, the Indian people, realized your intentions, we rose to do battle, to defend our nations, our homes, our food, our lives. And for our efforts we are labelled savages and our battles are called massacres.

And when our primitive weapons could not match those which you

had perfected through centuries of wars, we realized that peace could not be won, unless our mass destruction took place. And so we turned to treaties. And this time, we ran into your cunning trickery. And we lost our lands, our freedom and were confined to reservations. And we are held in contempt.

"As long as the Sun shall rise . . ." For you, White Man, these are words without meaning.

White Man, there is much in the deep, simple wisdom of our forefathers. We were here for centuries. We kept the land, the waters, the air clean and pure, for our children and for our children's children.

Now that you are here, White Man, the rivers bleed with contamination. The winds moan with the heavy weight of pollution in the air. The land vomits up the poisons which have been fed into it. Our Mother Earth is no longer clean and healthy. She is dying.

White Man, in your greedy rush for money and power, you are destroying. Why must you have power over everything? Why can't you live in peace and harmony? Why can't you share the beauty and the wealth which Mother Earth has given us?

You do not stop at confining us to small pieces of rock and muskeg. Where are the animals of the wilderness to go when there is no more wilderness? Why are the birds of the skies falling to their extinction? Is there joy for you when you bring down the mighty trees of our forests? No living thing seems sacred to you. In the name of progress, everything is cut down. And progress means only profits.

White man, you say that we are a people without dignity. But when we are sick, weak, hungry, poor, when there is nothing for us but death, what are we to do? We cannot accept a life which has been imposed on us.

You say that we are drunkards, that we live for drinking. But drinking is a way of dying. Dying without enjoying life. You have given us many diseases. It is true that you have found immunizations for many of these diseases. But this was done more for your own benefit. The worst disease, for which there is no immunity, is the disease of alcoholism. And you condemn us for being its easy victims. And those who do not condemn us weep for us and pity us.

So, we the Indian people, we are still dying. The land we lost is dying, too.

White Man, you have our land now.

Respect it. As we once did.

Take care of it. As we once did.

Love it. As we once did.

White Man, our wisdom is dying. As we are. But take heed, if Indian wisdom dies, you, White Man, will not be far behind.

So weep not for us.

Weep for yourselves.

And for your children.

And for their children.

Because you are taking everything today.

And tomorrow, there will be nothing left for them.

Cheryl had become more and more emotional as she went on. When she finished, we sat in silence. The only sounds were those of the crickets. Somewhere in the distance, a child was crying.

Finally I said, "I can see why they said it was controversial. I think it's powerful." We sat in silence for a few more minutes. "At the same time, though, I think you put too much blame on white men for everything. The Indian people did allow themselves to be treated like children. They should have stood up for their rights instead of letting themselves be walked on. You know what I mean?"

"Yeah?" Cheryl shot back in a challenging voice. "Where did it get the Métis?"

"But what exactly is it the Métis want? To live like Indians on reservations? To be dependent of the governments and therefore the white people? You once said the Métis people were an independent breed, freedom lovers."

"I still maintain that. But we don't have that kind of life." Cheryl added as an afterthought, "Because we don't have very many choices.

"Besides, that piece was mostly to warn those in control that they are going too fast. I'd like them to slow down. Let's enjoy life, give our children hope for tomorrow and get rid of those bloody clouds of bombs hanging over us all."

From *In Search of April Raintree* by Beatrice Culleton (1983).

Detail from '*Food Bank*' (*2nd State*) by Marvin Francis, 2004. Charcoal on paper.

TOMSON HIGHWAY

The four-storey façade of glass and concrete, giant chandeliers, crimson carpet, swirling silver lettering over its entrance—the Jubilee Concert Hall. Like blackflies in June, ticket buyers clustered around the box-office wickets. Between them and Jeremiah's bus stood a Plexiglas-covered display stand bearing the image of an exotic olive-complexioned man in a black tuxedo, a grand piano at his fingertips.

Tonight!
Vladimir Ashkenazy,
Russian pianist extraordinaire
With the Winnipeg Symphony Orchestra
Piano Concerto in E-minor by Frédéric Chopin

Into the curve of the propped-up piano top drifted, teetering dangerously on the white high heels, a reflection of the Indian woman in soiled white polyester.

A car came by that would have looked at home framed by the Californian surf and sunset: open convertible, white chrome gleaming. Four teenaged men with Brylcreamed hair lounged languidly inside, crotches thrust shamelessly, and laughed and puffed at cigarettes and sucked at bottles of nameless liquids.

"Hey, babe!" they hooted smoothly to the polyester Indian princess, "wanna go for a nice long ride?"

A brief verbal sparring followed, from Jeremiah's perspective, in pantomime. Then the princess stepped into the roofless car and the bus pulled forward.

TOMSON HIGHWAY was born at Maria Lake, Manitoba, on December 6, 1951. His father, Joe Highway, was a champion dogsled racer. Tomson attended a residential school at The Pas and received a Bachelor of Music degree and a BA from the University of Western Ontario. His play *The Rez Sisters* (1986) was a hit and he wrote several other plays. His novel *Kiss of the Fur Queen* (1998) is largely set in Winnipeg.

Gallantly, though not easily, Jeremiah left the episode behind him. Until one week later, he thought he saw the woman's picture on the back page of the *Winnipeg Tribune:* the naked body of Evelyn Rose McCrae—long-lost daughter of Mistik Lake—had been found in a ditch on the city's outskirts.

From *Kiss of the Fur Queen* by Tomson Highway (1998).

Sophisticates drinking wine at the opening of the Concert Hall, 1967. University of Manitoba Archives and Special Collections, Winnipeg Tribune Collection, 18-1486-42.

MARVIN FRANCIS

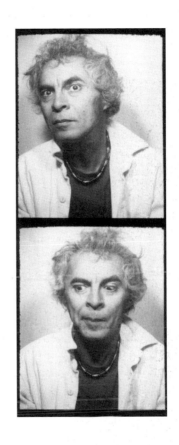

clown: time for the city
me: that is where I live
the city band

cig poem at the fix

Talk to 70s main street stories
Free for all, free for nobody, bar brawls
Cops too smart, too scared, to go inside
If U made it out you got arrested
So U fight your way to that corner, that desperate corner
People milling main street style
Shark circling   rolling drunks
Getting that role back all in the same night
70s main line town
some way how vibes alive
main event Saturday night
cruise crowds leather   cruise broken glass
fix that thought   fix that cigarette
talk of main

albert street
fix
cig poem

From *city treaty* by Marvin Francis (2002).

MARVIN FRANCIS was born in Alberta and lived in many places across the country. He received an MA from the University of Manitoba. His first collection of poetry, *city treaty* (2002), won him an award as Manitoba's most promising writer. He died on January 8, 2005.

YVONNE JOHNSON

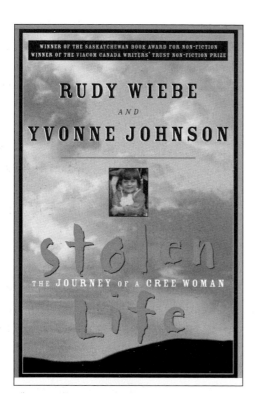

Compared with Butte, Winnipeg was a huge city, with all the extremes of society from the very rich to the poorest possible, and right at the bottom was a thick layer of Indians. Off Main, in the seventies, you could live for weeks and not see a White except for an owner or a bartender or a cop. If you wanted to go Indian, Canada, and Winnipeg especially, was the place. I had no idea there were so many Indians in the world, whole bars full of nothing but Indians, expecially the day the welfare cheques arrived. Karen was living with Gil, Kathy was living with Dan, both Natives, and Minnie was still somewhere in Alberta, and Perry with Dad in Butte. I stayed low, venturing out for no more than chips and gravy. The top song then was "Hot Summer in the City," and it fit, I guess. I knew how to be quiet, become a shadow, quite still, cross my arms and legs and stare at one spot, shut my body down, but I also learned how to deal wth two situations where I was vulnerable. One was when I walked alone: I learned to put on what I thought of as "the Johnson strut," long smooth strides, not running but gliding along really fast, I'd be gone before you knew it, a straight-ahead "don't fuck with me" walk.

The other situation was when I danced. I loved dancing, I'd become one with the music. In Canada women often danced with women, so it was simple to find a partner and I'd just disappear into that endless rhythm and movement. If no one jarred me I could dance all night. There were never any live bands or dance floors in the bars in Butte, but here there were many and they were one big reason I got addicted to skid-row Winnipeg.

We Johnson sisters dancing together would clean up a dance floor: everyone sitting around, watching us. They were used to old, slow waltz-style stuff, but we shook them up with American Bandstand style; I personally liked Soul Train music. Then when I turned seventeen, 4 October 1978, Mom decided we'd all go drinking together at the Savoy Hotel. She asked me to do the robot

Above left: Cover of *Stolen Life: the journey of a Cree woman.*

Dreary Winnipeg scene. University of Manitoba Archives and Special Collections, Winnipeg Tribune Collection, 18-6475-83.

dance; I could do it perfectly—I'd had enough practice all my life!—head and arms and hair dangling slack, moving like a mindless, completely controlled robot. Mom loved seeing me do that dance, so I danced for my mother. I was wearing all white, and Calvin (or Aaron—he used both names for welfare or unemployment-insurance scams) was at our table. Mom had once lived with him; he'd left, but now he'd showed up again, a romance for Mom that my presence in her home didn't fit with very well. While I did the robot dance, Calvin started a bar fight.

Last call had been made as the lights flicked off and on and he wanted to impress Mom, so he yelled out his order with all the rest. I don't think he'd ever ordered in his life, he was a living mooch, he lived mostly at the Sally Ann, and the waiters thought him a joke and didn't listen. Calvin had a head like a rock, and when a short waiter passed with an empty tray, to attract his attention he head-butted him and laid him out.

When the waiter got up off the floor, he banged Calvin with the butt of his own to the forehead. Calvin scrambled up, grabbed the waiter's hair with both hands, and smashed him dead centre. So the fight was on, Indians against the world, one entire side of the bar was breaking up. I tried to keep guys off Mom, but she was already fighting. Then the bartender cut the lights. In the dark there was screaming, tables and chairs crashing; when the lights came back on, the waiters and bouncers were yelling at everyone to leave, outa here, it's over! I was heading for the front door fast when the nasty short waiter shoved the firedoor open and threw me out across the alley against the brick wall. And there were the cops with nightsticks—they called them "Indian licorice sticks"—rushing us.

They slammed me over the trunk of a cop car with my arm twisted behind my back, and then more cars arrived fast as the Indians shot out of the door, and they clubbed them into a heap on the pavement—Winnipeg cops seemed to love caving in Indian heads, and I was just lucky being thrown out first—finally they threw me into the cruiser. Then Mom came out and I watched them beat my mother.

Her knees never buckled. She had two cops literally hanging on her arms, clubbing her with nightsticks. I tried to kick out the window to help her—my sad life with break-proof glass!—I was scared to death for her. They were breaking her arms back, pounding her head. She was clubbed on the forehead, and her face squashed down onto the trunk, but she twisted around and yelled, "Vonnie! Stay in the car!" when they got her cuffed, but the door was locked, I couldn't get out anyway, and a special car drove up just for her, and they stuffed a lot of people, most of them bleeding, into the back with me. They pulled us out inside the basement of the Remand Centre on Princess Street, I guess there were too many for the cop-shop cells, and there I saw them hauling Mom handcuffed into an elevator.

She shouted at me, "Just shut up, do as they say," before the doors slammed on her.

From *Stolen Life* by Rudy Wiebe and Yvonne Johnson (1998).

GORDON SINCLAIR

GORDON SINCLAIR Jr. is a city columnist with the *Winnipeg Free Press*. He was born and grew up in Winnipeg, where his father was also a newspaperman with the *Free Press*. His first book, *Cowboys and Indians: The Shooting of J.J. Harper*, won three awards, including the inaugural Carol Shields Winnipeg Book Award in 2000, and the 1999 Arthur Ellis Crime Writers of Canada Award for Best Non-Fiction Book. He also won the National Newspaper Award for column writing in 1989 for a series of columns, including one on his investigation of the Harper case.

At midnight on March 9 the sky was clear and the wind was blowing gently through the centre of the city. There are two centres to Winnipeg. Just over a kilometre east of the Legislature lies The Forks, where the Red and Assiniboine rivers converge. The Forks is the historic centre of the city. It was the meeting and trading place of Aboriginal peoples, and the site of the first fort built when the first white explorer arrived 250 years earlier. A railway station followed, and tracks were laid across the lacerated Indian land, like steel stitches. The Forks is now the city's most popular tourist attraction.

The other centre of the city lies a kilometre north of The Forks, where two streets intersect to form the coldest and windiest corner on the continent. Portage and Main is the symbolic heart of the business community whose office towers, viewed from certain angles, give Winnipeg a big-city look.

A few blocks north of Portage and Main, one of the country's saddest, most sordid streets starts in front of City Hall and then crawls for ten blocks past the railway lines that separate the north end from the city centre. In 1988 North Main Street was a grungy gauntlet of skid-row hotels, pawnshops, soup kitchens, and detox centres. Winnipeggers, the kind who locked their car doors as they drove past, and cursed at the drunks wandering obliviously across their paths, saw only Aboriginal faces on North Main Street. To them it was the biggest urban "reserve" in Canada. In 1986 the census reported there were nearly 28,000 Aboriginal people in Winnipeg. The migration from the reserves had begun slowly after the Second World War. Most came to the city looking for jobs and most were women who found them cleaning homes or working in restaurants. The men who followed them worked in unskilled jobs. In those years, Indians were prohibited from drinking alcohol in public places. Tommy Prince, the country's most decorated Aboriginal war hero, couldn't get a drink in a Legion Hall. In the early 1960s, the prohibition was lifted. A decade later, having pawned his war medals, Tommy Prince died a destitute drunk.

From *Cowboys and Indians* by Gordon Sinclair (1999).

Police checkpoint on Winnipeg street. University of Manitoba Archives and Special Collections, Winnipeg Tribune Collection, 18-6254-118.

Portage Avenue, 1975. University of Manitoba Archives and Special Collections, Winnipeg Tribune Collection, 18-6261-159.

THE NEW METROPOLIS

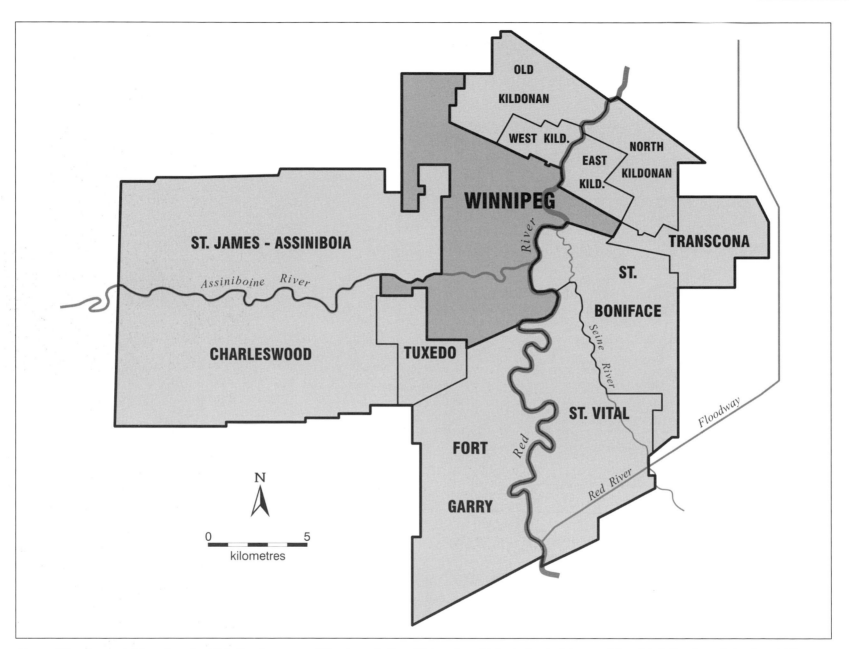

Above: Winnipeg neighbourhoods, 1971. Previous page: Winnipeg skyline. University of Manitoba Archives and Special Collections, Winnipeg Tribune Collection, 18-6261-157.

GEORGE AMABILE

PR*AIRIE*

a light word
filled with wistful spokes
of sun through the overcast at dusk
or smoke totems bent at the top
wisping away into beige emulsions

an earth word
a moist darkness turning
stones and roots
fossils and tiny lives
up to the sun

a watery word
mirage and heat lightning
steadied by pewter barns
where whole towns float in a lilting haze
and rumors of rain rise from the rapeseed
lakes

a flame shaped word
a ragged mane blowing
for miles across dry grass
lighting the night like fired breath
out of the old testament

a word with air
in its belly that howls
for hours or days and dries
the memory of soft conversation
to wheatdust under the tongue

like the distance we've come
to stand here in the sky at the top of the world

From *Open Country* by George Amabile (1976).

GEORGE AMABILE was born May 29, 1936, in Jersey City, New York. He received an MA from the University of Minnesota and a PhD from the University of Connecticut. He came to Canada in 1963 and taught at the University of Manitoba until his retirement. He founded the literary journals *The Far Point* and *Northern Light*. His collection of poetry, *The Presence of Fire* (1982), won the Canadian Author's Association Award for Poetry.

DAVID ARNASON

DAVID ARNASON was born in Gimli, Manitoba, on May 23, 1940. He received a BA and MA from the University of Manitoba, and a PhD from the University of New Brunswick. He has written poetry, stage plays, short stories, and novels. Since 1972, he has taught at the University of Manitoba.

MARSH BURNING

after the long rolling hills of Ontario
lake and river
hill and river
lake
we swept over Manitoba's border
down the undulating road
past the burned out forest deadfall
now greening again
and only a few skeletal trees
to remind us of fire
memory singing now
we slid into
fields
green and yellow
barley wheat and oats
flax the colour a lake should be
poles that vee'd to the horizon
a high sky with clouds
massed and turbulent
past the elevator at Dufresne

we slid faster and faster
the road becoming flatter as we moved
as if the car no longer needed power
but could glide
did glide
into the heart of that prairie
into Winnipeg
into home

Continued

leaning against the balcony
on the fourteenth floor of the Regency Towers
Winnipeg spread out before us this night
an electric map of irrational ganglia
I am tempted to jump
to hurl myself into the centre of this space
and never land
but we are drinking Tequila
and making plans
our desires sharpened by alcohol

the room loses focus
but next year is hard and clear
Greece Turkey the Isle of Crete
the Parthenon the hot Mediterranean sun

all stronger than the tang of lemons
the soft bland taste of salt

From *Marsh Burning* by David Arnason (1980).

Winnipeg high-rise, c. 1970. University of
Manitoba Archives and Special Collections,
Winnipeg Tribune Collection, 18-2332-001.

DENNIS COOLEY

DENNIS COOLEY was born in Estevan, Saskatchewan, on August 27, 1944. He received a BA and MA from the University of Saskatchewan and his PhD from the University of Rochester. He moved to Winnipeg in 1973 and has taught at the University of Manitoba ever since. He has published several books of poetry and criticism. His best-known work is the long poem *Bloody Jack* (1984).

THEY LEAVE THEIR TRACES

Every spring
Our back yard throws up new wonders
Old wire stones of all sizes nails hundreds of nails
(mostly bent) a buckle chunks of wood one head from a
sledge hammer a porcelain knob pieces of china some with
blue markings buttons cans that look like theyre eaten
by metal moths hunks of concrete pieces of what looks like
black top bolts some with nuts some without old posts a
few coins badly decayed marbles there are a few marbles
bits of brick and crumbled masonry straps of iron broken
most often at the bolt holes something we take to be animal
teeth a spoon with no handle cracked vertebrae

& once a horse shoe leapt like a frog into the air
& we put it by the shed to save lids from tins & jars rivets
coloured bottles pieces of rope wed find unidentifiable
bars of metal squirms of wire for maybe chickens or plaster
screws caked with rust a spoon Diane found a spoon one time

& theres one spot at the top of the garden
where the garden tractor grinds &
grinds on something hard
only it never appears

we put them in piles
these strange articles
              every spring
the leavings of lives dribble into ours
a little of nouns
  refuse to speak

once when we first started the garden I pulled some
flattened eavestroughing out some times there are
handles from cups lengths of chain in one corner one
time there was this huge lid for a barrel & we chopped
it out 2 feet deep Diane & I with a pick in the mud
we pried it free & we squashed it as much as we cld
for the garbage

Blacksmith and giant horseshoe. Archives of
Manitoba, N2004.

this place they sd once was a blacksmiths
at the head of a ferry where
Riel waited for MacDougall
& theres a sign just down Pembina
by a pile of rubble
that tells about it.

From *Bloody Jack* by Dennis Cooley (1984).

LARRY KROTZ

LARRY KROTZ was born in Gowanstown, Ontario, and attended Glendon College, York University. He lived in Winnipeg for many years before moving to Toronto. He has worked as a writer, journalist, and documentary producer. His novel *Shutter Speed* (1988) is a picture of urban Manitoba.

By reputation, Winnipeg was the unadventurous centre of a careful, unenthusiastic country. Demographic reports defined the city as 'stale', a land of missed opportunities and exaggerated pretensions. If fortunes were slow, the city burghers frequently resorted to jingles to try to turn things around, to bring the world galloping to their door (Winnerpeg, some brilliant light had decided to call it). But for Danny, in his current mood, it acquired a magic of infinite dimensions. It was a house of mirrors, an orchestra, a symphony. "Strike up the band!" he wanted to shout. "Isn't this wonderful? So many human beings with so many histories, so many genealogical, chromosomatic lines, so many misunderstandings, so many possibilities, so many energies, so many fantasies, so many dreams ... doesn't it make you want to shout?"

He started off on a walk with no particular destination. The city went on forever, following its rivers, its avenues, its bridges, its railroad tracks. At its outer reaches, in every direction, were split-level houses on manicured boulevards, houses with wet bars in the basement and video games for the kids. He turned in the other direction, toward the older city, and after 20 minutes was walking under the overhang of old buildings, elderly warehouses with theatre schools and gung-fu studios on their upper floors. Here and there bright new owners were attempting to make even more dramatic transformations, and sandblasters wearing goggles and masks like spacemen hung from ladders while they tortured the grime off warehouses, trying to convert them into new chic shops and apartments. He stood still on a street corner and watched and listened to the hum of the city. The city was a chaotic mill but it could be, he thought, not a chaos but a ballet. He pictured two directions simultaneously on his downtown street corner and let his mind gallop into a private fantasy of a ballet. A ballet of churches and beer halls and slaughterhouses, union halls and labourers pas de deux-ing with hard hats and lunch buckets; a ballet of girls in insurance offices and young men in banks, salesmen in brilliantly blinking suits and car dealers lining the avenues. His mind choreographed elderly women arriving at first bell to Eaton's and real dancers, their bodies taut, emerging from the studios of the real ballet. He imagined the dance of dentist's offices, juvenile delinquents toughing it out in front of arcades, and crazy old men selling the *Free Press* along Portage Avenue by yelling out World War Two headlines; BMWs emerging from the underground parking garages of tall apartment buildings and Indians poking along the banks of the river, pretending that they were back up north in Shamattawa. The music of the street was that of cops in squeaky shoes and, in office buildings, the hum of photocopying machines and civil servants waiting for coffee time. He loved the city, he loved the streets; his heart welled up with affection for all the people he didn't even know. He thought of the places where he found them.

From *Shutter Speed* by Larry Krotz (1988).

Dancers from the Royal Winnipeg Ballet—Gaile Petursson, Julie Whittaker, Sheila Long. University of Manitoba Archives and Special Collections, Tribune Collection, 18-4985-177.

ROBERT KROETSCH

ROBERT KROETSCH was born in Heisler, Alberta, in 1927. He received his BA from the University of Alberta in 1948 and his MA from Middlebury College in Vermont. He received a PhD in creative writing from the University of Iowa. His postmodern novels, such as *What the Crow Said* (1983), and his long poem *Seed Catalogue* (1986) have had a significant influence on other prairie writers.

THE WINNIPEG ZOO

yes I am here, exhausted, a wreck, unable
to imagine the act of writing, unable to imagine

I am here, it is quiet, I am exhausted from
moving, we must take care of our stories

the moving is a story, we must take care, I am
here, I shall arrive, I am arriving, I too

have waited, the way in is merely the way,
she takes her lovers, reader, listen, be careful

she takes her lovers one by one to the Winnipeg
zoo, she winds her hair on her fingers, the hook

in the ceiling holds the plant, the ivy climbs
to the floor, must in the end

of winter, the ride to the zoo, the sun on the
man at the gate, the hair wound on her fingers

she takes her lovers, first, the startled boy
stares at the pink flamingos, they rest, folding

one leg at a time, the standing boy, she returns
alone from the Winnipeg zoo, her brown eyes

misting into calm, the hook in the ceiling
holds the plant, what matters is all that matters

Section from *Completed Field Notes* by Robert Kroetsch (1989).

The bear pits at Assiniboine Park. Archives of Manitoba, Barbara Johnstone Collection, 192.

WAYNE TEFS

WAYNE TEFS was born in 1947 and grew up in northwestern Ontario. He did his BA and PhD at the University of Manitoba and his MA at the University of Toronto. He has taught at the University of Regina and the University of Manitoba, and at St. John's Ravenscourt in Winnipeg. He is a prolific novelist, writing stories and mysteries set in Winnipeg and northern Ontario.

This neighborhood is called Woodydell. Isolated by the river on one side and perimeter dikes on the others, Woodydell is not the most pricey neighborhood in the city, but it appeals to ecologists and New Left holdovers from the sixties, including, Michael has come to accept over the past decade, himself. It's a planned community. Diagonal sidewalks converge on a central park where children wing from wooden gymnasiums and then scoot down walkways to homes renovated according to *Architectural Digest*. Mary gushes over Woodydell. No cars, no crowds. *Gorgeous,* she calls it, one of her favorite words. Woodydell boasts ten acres of parks, a community club on the river, and forty species of trees. Volvos, Saabs, Subarus. Strangely, Michael feels at home here among civil servants, architects, and stockbrokers—types he once snubbed, suspecting their trimmed beards and button-down morality. Now he chats them up at the health-foods counter and shares tubes of Primo Caulk in the fall. Happy. Fat. He likes the trim wives who ferry their kids from Highland dance to ringette in Suburbans. His neighbors come over on warm summer nights and they play canasta and listen to old records. They bask in the glow of good scotch, the glow of middle age, the glow of success. Michael signs petitions protecting Woodydell from freeways, he referees little league soccer, he sprays his trees for bark beetles. With his neighbors Michael agrees that if it weren't for Dutch elm disease Woodydell would be perfect. Like them he votes Liberal and wears toe rubbers over his loafers during spring thaw.

And jogs. It's supposed to keep his weight down, but it isn't working. So far all he's got from running is pain. Cramps, stitches, a twinge he hasn't felt in his knee since the days when he played high-school basketball in Belvu. Was it really thirty years ago? Lately there've been spasms in the back. Still, they're nothing compared to the gut-aches he gets brooding about Angela.

He feels sweat on his brow. He wonders if it's the heat, or the terror of seeing the bikers, or nearly killing the man on Pembina. Or Angela. Coal-black hair, black nails, the scent of mint on her breath, the scent of sexual excitement and danger in every twitch of her young body. Angela. Some things are better not thought about. Michael closes his eyes and listens to the rattling leaves. It feels hot even though it's been raining. But this heat is good for him. It burns fat. Which he's got a lot of, now that he's living the soft life—teaching graduate courses, pecking out his newspaper column. Life's treated him good, better than he deserves, and he's thickened to 230 pounds, as heavy as when he left his first wife. In those days he guzzled Johnny Walker like he owned an interest in the company. He smiles. The idea appeals to him, owning shares in a big conglomerate. Seagrams gained two bucks last week after the CEO announced a move into coolers. You could do worse than put your money in booze.

From *The Canasta Players* by Wayne Tefs (1990).

Residential Wildwood Park. University of Manitoba Archives and Special Collections, Winnipeg Tribune Collection, 18-6166-1.

CAROL SHIELDS

CAROL SHIELDS was born in Oak Park, Illinois, on June 2, 1935. She received a BA at Hanover College and her MA from the University of Ottawa. She moved with her husband to Winnipeg, where she taught at the University of Manitoba before retiring to Victoria in 1999. Her novel *The Stone Diaries* (1994) won a Pulitzer Prize, a Governor General's Award, and the McNally Robinson Book of the Year Award, and was short-listed for the Booker Prize in Britain. Much of her work is set in Winnipeg. She died on July 16, 2003.

"Let's hear those telephones ringing," Tom pleaded to his "Niteline" listeners on Monday night. "Today's our annual roundup of civic affirmation. It's booster night. Are you ready out there? Okay then. 'I love Winnipeg because—'"

At first the calls dribbled in.

"Well, it so happens I love Winnipeg," the first caller said, "because my roots are here." He interrupted himself with an eager piercing laugh. "This is not a city of transients. You just plain old-fashioned live here. And so does everyone you know."

"I don't love Winnipeg, I adore Winnipeg." The voice was boozy, female, full of squawks. "And I'll tell you why. I like seasons. Have you been out to the west coast? They've got one season out there, the rainy season. Gets boring. Bo-ring."

"I don't love Winnipeg at all," the third caller said. "Everyone here is trying their damndest to love it, that's the whole problem. Methinks they doth protest too much. We've got a lousy climate here; we've got to grit our teeth and put up with it. So let's can all this you-know-what about loving it here. Let's be honest for a change."

"Hey, Tom, you there? You mind if I reply to Miss Sourpuss, your previous caller? She's forgetting what this city offers. I'm talking sports, entertainment. I'm talking great movies, and the biggest shopping mall this side of Edmonton."

"Go ahead, caller," Tom said. "Are you there?"

"My permanent home is in Winnipeg at the moment, but I've got a transfer coming up and I'm going to be putting my house on the market. If anyone out there's interested in a fantastic bargain, split-level, three bedrooms—"

"I love Winnipeg because the people here are the salt of the earth. You walk down Portage and you get smiles from everyone, even the cops. I do wish they'd stop their scrapping on City Council, though. We've got some real nerds on City Council, one or two in particular, real dinosaurs. Okay if I mention their names on the air?"

"Maybe we should just leave it at that," Tom suggested, giving Ted Woloschuk the wind-up signal.

"I love Winnipeg," the final caller said, "but I'd love it more if we had a few more heated bus-shelters. It's summer, but I'm starting to dread winter already, standing out there every morning on Henderson Highway and freezing my buns off. Otherwise this is paradise. I mean it. It's heaven."

From *The Republic of Love* by Carol Shields (1992).

Radio announcer Bert Perlman. Archives of Manitoba, Jewish Historical Society Collection, 855.

DAVID WILLIAMSON

Bob Jenkins, Winnipeg high school principal, dabbler in the stock market, husband, father of two grownup kids, owner of an overly affectionate golden retriever, wakes early one Saturday morning in February to find no one beside him in the queen-sized double bed. He remembers that his wife Barb is away this weekend; she's down in Grand Forks, North Dakota, with some of her women friends, curling and shopping.

This is Barb's idea of a treat, to be away with other women, drinking scotch, telling raunchy jokes, playing bridge in her nightie. She says she's going to buy some clothes while she's down there, but she's not going to smuggle anything across the border. Her friends can lie to the Customs officers if they want to, but Barb's going to declare everything and pay the duty.

Jenkins wonders, Should he get up or should he stay in bed?

Continued

"Wally's the most androgynous man I know," Linda said when she introduced him to Joyce. Wally blushed; he wondered if Linda wasn't over-selling him.

They were on the promenade deck of the *Lord Selkirk* cruise ship, sailing slowly up the Red River one evening in June. A local writers' group was sponsoring this cruise, inviting people to meet the various Manitoba authors who were on board. Wally, a history prof at the University of Manitoba, did a lot of writing but had not published anything beyond some academic papers ("Riel: Romantic or Rotter?") and a few book reviews. At the invitation of Linda and her guidance counsellor husband, Emil, Wally had come along on the cruise to *meet* Manitoba authors, not *be* one. When he learned that Joyce, the Friesens' other guest, ran a computer store, he asked her all about word processors. He felt it was time he bought one. He was sure that all that stood between him and literary success was mastering an IBM-PC or an Apple. He hated to admit it but he still wrote his first drafts long-hand.

That evening, with the summer breeze in their hair, Wally and Joyce became so engrossed in each other they practically ignored the Friesens, to say nothing of the Manitoba authors.

From *Accountable Advances* by Dave Williamson (1994).

Boating on a Winnipeg river. University of Manitoba Archives and Special Collections, Winnipeg Tribune Collection, 18-3413-19.

CATHERINE HUNTER

CATHERINE HUNTER was born in Regina, Saskatchewan, in 1957. She grew up in Winnipeg. She received her PhD from the University of Victoria. She teaches creative writing at the University of Winnipeg. She has published several collections of poetry, among them *Lunar Wake* (1994), and several mystery novels.

WHY I CAME TO LIVE IN ST. BONIFACE

because it was summertime
you played the fiddle
a cat lay over the doorsill, dreaming
she was neither inside or out

because you filled the house with jazz
and with tomatoes—the bright sound
of their ripe skins bursting, the scent
of peanut oil

because you concealed from me the fact
that the walls of your house are an illusion
that butterflies and squirrels move through them
that a kitchen ladle can find its way
down to the lilac roots at the bottom of the garden
with no help from a human hand

because you didn't tell me about the wind
how it lets in everything, dead lives, spiders
absent-mindedness, the mist off the river
i thought you said you lived
by the sane river

you'd lie beside me on the bed, turn your face
to the wall and see the seven directions
of the neighbourhood, every yard on the street,
bulbs under the grass, the sky

you saw our daughter and you
picked up your fiddle, you baked bread
you brewed beer, you danced
the dance of conspiracy, seduction, *the house*
you said *will make room* and I joined in
we chanted *room room room* the rafters parted
like pelvic bones, door frames bulged outward
our daughter turned her unborn head, listening

we didn't tell her
about the wind

From *Lunar Wake* by Catherine Hunter (1994).

The cramped front gardens were carefully tended and filled with shrubs, mostly bleeding hearts and azaleas. Here in Wolseley, the tall houses were built so closely together that their upper eaves overlapped, and the huge American elms on either side of the street had spread so wide that their branches touched each other high above the middle of the road. Sunlight was at a premium, and every available patch of sunny ground was crowded with plantings. Avid

Protecting the Wolseley Elm. University of Manitoba Archives and Special Collections, Winnipeg Tribune Collection, 18-5660-11.

gardeners, frustrated with their own shady yards, would plant anywhere they could. They dug up the wide grass boulevards between the sidewalk and the road, and seeded them with marigolds and oregano and sometimes even tomatoes, though that was risky—too tempting for passersby. Tulips and daffodils bloomed around the bus stop, and a morning-glory vine was beginning its long climb up the bus stop sign. Along the curb Sarah recognized the green shoots of peonies, shasta daisies, and day lilies. Yes, summer was coming to Winnipeg. Summer, and the Manitoba Marathon, which Sarah wouldn't be running. Her arms ached, but she pressed on, determined to make it to Westminster Avenue.

From *The Dead of Midnight* by Catherine Hunter (2001).

MEEKA WALSH

Meeka Walsh was born and raised in Winnipeg. She is the editor of the arts magazine *Border Crossings*, and is on the board of the National Gallery of Canada. She has published a memoir, *Ordinary Magic* (1989), and a collection of stories, *The Garden of Earthly Intimacies* (1996).

It was February and no one moves to Winnipeg in February but she didn't know this. All she knew was that in New York, without light, she would disappear. The atlas hadn't mentioned that in February the sun would be low in the sky for much of the time on either side of noon. The sky, as noted, was blue, such a blue that she could only open her mouth wide and drink it in a bubble that hurt her chest with joy and excess. The atlas hadn't said—or maybe she'd neglected to read that everything, everything would be covered in a crust of white and that this white was such a white that even after the sun slid from its high point her eyes—two apertures fixed at open—recorded the dazzle and stored it so that she read without turning on the overhead light, late into the nights. So ready and so sensitive to light was she that she was able to perceive that day by day each one began later. So the light stretched. In this light, this extraordinary sweet and liquid light she expected to find the city of Winnipeg filled with artists. In time she came to recognize that this was so.

Through habit she located herself at the city's centre in an area which, if the city were more crowded and jammed with commerce, would be as like SoHo as any other. Named for its history as a centre of trade it was called The Exchange District and here, in an old building, she made her home. Now she lived on the fifth floor of a red brick building but there were no floors above hers and no buildings so near that blocked the light that washed through the high arched windows or ranged along the other two walls of what she knew now was her home.

Close by was a long wide street, so wide she might have thought she was in Paris and that this was the Champs Elysées, so generously did she wish to see, and her eyes still dazzled by light. This was Main Street she was told and it ran north and south on an uninterrupted axis. And here, at its middle was another wide, wide street and this one ran from east to west and it was named Portage Avenue and where they met was a star and when she stood in this star late one night after all the traffic had stopped she felt to be in a magnetic centre, this Portage and Main, which set her very being right, pulling and pushing her awkward misalignments until she was steady as the tumblers in an oiled lock.

From "Light Reading," by Meeka Walsh in *Prairie Fire* 20, 2 (1999).

The Artspace Building, 100 Arthur Street, c. 1980s. Courtesy The Manitoba Writers' Guild.

ARMIN WIEBE

ARMIN WIEBE was born in Altona, Manitoba, and studied at the universities of Winnipeg and Manitoba. He has taught school in Manitoba and in the Northwest Territories. His novels, set in the fictional Mennonite community of Gutenthal, are highly comic. His best-known works are *The Salvation of Yasch Siemens* (1984) and *The Second Coming of Yeeat Shpanst* (1995). In 2004 he won both the Margaret Laurence Award for Fiction and the McNally Robinson Book of the Year Award for his novel *Tatsea* (2003).

"Winnipeg in the cellar."

I know she means to Eaton's and so we drive through all the cars with the yellow Honey Wagon behind and I drive real slow because I don't want to hook anything on and I don't want to drive any red lights through. So cars are honking us behind and it's almost like a wedding they so much noise make but I just drive slow because I know the way. I was here last year once. And we get there, too. But the guy in that parking place where you can drive your car upstairs doesn't like it when I want to park the Honey Wagon in there, but I show him that the tank isn't so high that it will hook on the roof and so he lets me through because there are already twenty cars honking after us. But the parking place is real full and we have to drive all the way up the roof before we can find enough room.

Oata is hungry now already and my stomach is hanging crooked, too, so after we go through the tunnel that is way up over the street we look in Eaton's for a place to eat. Oata sees it first, the sign grill room, and so we go in there and sit by one of those white tables. Some books with leather covers say what you can eat there and Oata says that she wants to try some of this French stuff and when she shows me where it says "Filet Mignon" I almost fuhschluck myself because it will cost so much as two twenty-fours, but then I remember that Ha Ha gave me money so I say sure, and I snap my fingers like we always do in the Neche beer parlour and this old lady with a white paper crown on her head and red lipstick comes running over and I say, "Two fillet mig-nons please," and she writes with her little pencil on the little paper and she asks, "How do you want it done?" and I think a little bit and I say, "Cooked" and Oata shakes her head up and down to show that she wants hers cooked, too. And the lady says, "Soup or juice," and I say, "Both," and Oata wants it like that, too, but when the lady says, "What kind of dressing on your salad?" I don't know what to say so I ask, "What kind you got?" She says, "French, Italian, Thousand Islands, and Oil and Vinegar." So I say right away, "French," because we will eat French food, but Oata says, "Thousand Islands," and when the little old lady has gone away Oata says to me that she picked Thousand Islands because when she was twelve she found a pen pal once in the *Free Press Weekly Prairie Farmer* that was from Thousand Islands by Ontario and she would like to go visit there some time.

Well, the lady brings the soup and the juice first and we quickly drink the tomato juice because we are real thirsty already. Then we eat the soup and the lady has brought us some biscuits in little plastic bags, too, and Oata puts them in her pink purse so we can eat them if we get hungry in the store. The soup tastes pretty good, but the bowl is so small the spoon hardly fits in. Then the salad comes and my salad has this orange stuff poured on it and Oata's has some pinky stuff.

Then the Fillet Mig-non comes and all it is is some cow meat that isn't quite cooked because the blood still runs out and there is a big potato that is cooked with the peel on and then not even some gravy. But there is some butter so I smear it on the potato after I peel it and I say to Oata that at least they could the potatoes peel for us but she just smiles and I can see that she is happy for sure.

In Eaton's it is full with people, all women just, only some men, and you get almost dizzy trying to look them all on. Women with shorts on and red lips and toenails. Young thin girls with high heels and open toes and dresses that come only half to the knees or long dresses that they forgot to sew all the way up the sides so you can see the leg almost to the seat of knowledge. And one that we see when we go up the bale loader stairs has white pants on that are so tight and so thin that they look like they were painted on and you can see the red flowers on her underpants through the seat. And everyone has on lipstick, even old women like Muttachi. Then there aren't even enough live ones yet. They have all these big women dolls all over the place and some have nice clothes on, and some don't have any, and some just have legs and they are upside down and have double nylons on just. So many women a guy could go crazy in such a place.

But Oata has me by the hand and she pulls me from one thing to the other and we look at everything, and sometimes when we see something we know we say, "Look, that you can buy in Harder's store" or "Such they have at the Co-ops" or "Fuchtich Froese had such a cap on the picnic." We go all the floors through and we lauger ourselves good at the place where they just have panties and brassieres, so many colours yet like a whole crayon box full, and there is one of those women dolls that has on just a brassiere and panties that are made from soft fuzzy feathers like baby chicks have. And Oata says, "That would tickle, not?" And I tickle her a little bit on the side and she doesn't hit me with her pink purse.

We go all the floors up even to the last one where they have beds and such but we don't buy nothing and we start to go down. Then we get to the cellar, where we didn't go before and it's different from the other parts. There isn't so much lipstick here and not so many shorts and red toenails. And no women dolls. Soon I hear people talking Flat German, and I look and I see people from Gnadenthal, then by the shoes I see some from Winkler. By the soft ice cream and hot dog place, when we stop there for some, we see people from Reinland and Rosengart and we talk them on a little while. It seems like half the cellar is talking Flat German. But then everybody goes to Winnipeg in the cellar.

From *The Salvation of Yasch Siemens* by Armin Wiebe (1984).

MIRIAM TOEWS

MIRIAM TOEWS was born in Steinbach, Manitoba, in 1964. She received a BA from the University of Manitoba and a Bachelor of Journalism from the University of King's College. She received the John Hirsch Award for Most Promising Manitoba Writer in 1996 and the McNally Robinson Book of the Year Award for her novel *Boy of Good Breeding* (1998). Her novel *A Complicated Kindness* (2004) was nominated for the 2004 Giller Prize and won the Governor General's Award for fiction that same year.

The midwestern United States was starting to flood. Rivers were running over farmers' fields and into their homes. Entire towns were being threatened by swollen rivers. Major highways and bridges were being wiped out. It was only a matter of time before the Red and the Assiniboine, Winnipeg's rivers, would feel the pressure and begin to rise. With the rain came the mosquitoes. Every puddle, larger or small, became fertile breeding grounds for those damn bugs. Our children were covered in bites. Some were too young to spray with repellent because the chemicals in the spray seeped through the skin into their blood. Others had mothers who didn't believe in it. They tried to ward off the mosquitoes with home remedies, Avon's Skin So Soft and Citronella, but nothing worked. Soon some kids, especially the ones that were too young to slap mosquitoes off, had started a second layer of bites. Dill had three mosquito bites one on top of the other above his right eye. One morning he woke up and his eye was swollen shut.

We couldn't even open our windows, because the buggers managed to get through the miniscule holes in the screens, those that had them. At night you could hear the collective scratching of all of Half-a-Life's bite victims. We scratched until we bled. It was common for the kids to walk around with the dark bodies of mosquitoes squished onto their skin. They couldn't be bothered to flick them off anymore after they had slapped them. If the mosquito was slapped with a belly full of fresh blood, skin and clothing were stained. The walls in our apartments had ugly smears of dead mosquitoes. Large chunks of our days were devoted to tracking mosquitoes, creeping from room to room, standing on chairs and furniture, cornering them, and adding to their death toll. We were told by the experts on the six o'clock news to wear white long sleeves and pants. But it didn't matter what we wore. They still got through.

Even the animals were suffering. Farmers couldn't sell their meat for as much as they were used to. Big pork hams had ugly bites all over the skin and nobody wanted to buy them.

Terrapin advised us all to take an organic pill containing kelp and hyssop and tree bark. She said it would make our broken skin heal faster. People didn't want to go out for any reason, not even for beer.

From *Summer of My Amazing Luck* by Miriam Toews (1996).

Built in 1984, the giant mosquito monument at Komarno, Manitoba, is one of the world's largest mosquitoes. With a wingspan of almost five metres, the monument also functions as a weather vane. The word "komarno" means "mosquito" in Ukrainian. Courtesy Mhari Mackintosh.

JON PAUL FIORENTINO

JON PAUL FIORENTINO was born in Winnipeg and grew up in the suburb of Transcona. He won the University of Winnipeg
Writers Circle Prize. He has published
several collections of poetry, including
transcona fragments (2002).

TRANSCONA FRAGMENTS

ah good old ground tasting like invasive snow
salt reeling under exhaust (no matter the cost)
and don't forget to write from the east where
you will sit in a state of abandoned bliss stitched
to a street that hardly knows you

unpacking that metaphor the unkempt gravel
or tar of a transcona side street driving with your
third eye on the road splaying yourself out the side
window, with both eyes on what you know

that taste, that region: gravel, tar, spit leaves
of glass splinters on the dream road tin am radio
chevrolet and a block heater and an electric blanket
and a six pack for christmas

park on the frigid plain, dig a ditch round the city
plunge into floodway and dream headlong into traffic
as if you had the guts as if you ever had
the pleasure

under windows laced with the thickest frost
you ramble on about the weather and the family
and i'm almost lured into your language until i recoil
at the irrational flash of a police search light

we quickly clothe ourselves and turn down the heater
and turn up the radio and pretend to be innocents with
decorative smiles for the constable who was hoping
for something more cinematic

From *transcona fragments* by Jon Paul Fiorentino (2002).

Transcona main street, 1935. Archives of Manitoba, N19704.

SANDRA BIRDSELL

SANDRA BIRDSELL was born in Hamiota, Manitoba, on April 22, 1942. She was raised in Morris, Manitoba. She married and was a homemaker before returning to the University of Manitoba, where she studied creative writing with Robert Kroetsch. Her novels and short stories have received numerous awards, including both the Saskatchewan Book of the Year award and the McNally Robinson Book of the Year award. Her early stories, collected as *Agassiz Stories* (1987), are realist stories about women's lives in Winnipeg and rural Manitoba.

The western sky was ablaze with a hot pink that was reflected in the office buildings downtown and in the faces of the people around Emily as she allowed herself to be swept towards the sloped lawns of the Legislature and the sound of rap music. Her progress downtown had been delayed by a parade of tractors, farm machinery resembling space vehicles and lunar robots. The need to buy gas and find somewhere to park. Then she'd had to find a way around the police barricade at Memorial Boulevard and Portage Avenue, their attempt to prevent others from joining a party already in progress. The revellers, dancing in a fountain on Memorial, men naked to the waist, scantily dressed women, their faces and bodies painted in the red and white of the Canadian flag.

She elbowed and manoeuvred her way among the jostling and energized horde to the Osborne Street Bridge, clutching her bag against her body, grateful that she'd had the foresight to tuck several bills and a credit card into her brassiere before leaving the car. She was halfway across the bridge when familiar faces came towards her, the two occupants of the SUV, and their silver husky dog slinking along between them. Their faces lit up when they recognized her, the smaller man raising a beer in a salute, and for a moment Emily feared they might embrace her as though she were a long-lost friend.

"Some party," they said simultaneously, their grins too wide and eyes jittery. "Some poor bugger just got thrown off the bridge," the larger of the two men said. Emily saw the people lining the river's edge, a flotilla of boats idling nearby, the river patrol inching its way among them.

"They got him. He wasn't in for more than a few minutes. Hardly enough time to get wet," the smaller man said. Then he took a wineglass from his shirt pocket and pushed it into her hand. A souvenir from a bar, he explained, his hand shaking as he filled it with beer.

The river was swollen with rain and its current swift. She imagined the force of it, being pulled out to where the two rivers merged. She would tell Irene, that's how I feel. I feel caught, pulled, absorbed. Only, dear Irene of the sunny-side-up disposition would likely not understand. Irene had seen the photographs of Emily's house in its various stages of construction. She had been awed by the finished and furnished rooms, the efficient and beautiful kitchen with its centre island and stainless steel appliances, the rack of utensils, each with a particular purpose. A castle. You're living in a castle, Irene said without a trace of envy or malice. A minor castle, Emily admitted.

"*Je me souviens,*" the larger man said, a smirk twisting his face sideways. "It's likely the poor bugger's not going to forget this night, either. We got into an argument, and he lost."

From "Out Here," by Sandra Birdsell in *Praire Fire* 23,3 (2002).

Osborne Village, circa 1970s. University of Manitoba Archives and Special Collections, Winnipeg Tribune Collection, 18-4350-1.

JOHN SAMSON

JOHN SAMSON was born in Winnipeg on April 17, 1973. He attended Brock Corydon School and graduated from Kelvin High School. He played with the punk band Propaghandi and with the alternative band The Weakerthans. He is a member of Arbeiter Ring Publishing, a Winnipeg publishing company, and probably the most intellectual rock singer in North America.

ONE GREAT CITY

Late afternoon, another day is nearly done.
A darker gray is breaking through a lighter one.
A thousand sharpened elbows in the underground.
That hollow hurried sound of feet on polished floor,
and in the Dollar Store the clerk is closing up,
and counting Loonies, trying not to say,

"I hate Winnipeg."

The driver checks the mirror, seven minutes late.
The crowded riders' restlessness enunciates
that the Guess Who suck, the Jets were lousy anyway.
The same route every day.
And in the turning lane, someone's stalled again.
He's talking to himself,
and hears the price of gas repeat his phrase:

"I hate Winnipeg."

And up above us all, leaning into sky,
our Golden Business Boy
will watch the North End die,
and sing "I love this town,"
then let his arcing wrecking ball proclaim,

"I hate Winnipeg."

The Golden Boy. University of Manitoba
Archives and Special Collections, Winnipeg
Tribune Collection, 18-4311a-008.

BIBLIOGRAPHY

Amabile, George. "Prairie." In *Open Country*. Winnipeg: Turnstone Press Ltd., 1976.

Arnason, David. *Marsh Burning*. Winnipeg: Turnstone Press, 1980.

Begg, Alexander. *"Dot it Down": A Story of Life in the North-West*. Toronto: Toronto Reprint Library of Canadian Prose and Poetry, University of Toronto Press, 1973. First published in Toronto by Hunter, Rose & Company, 1871.

Beynon, Francis Marion. *Aleta Dey*. London: C.W. Daniel Ltd, 1919.

Birdsell, Sandra. "Out Here." *Prairie Fire* 23, 3 (2002).

Butler, William Francis. *The Great Lone Land: A Narrative of Travel and Adventure in the North-West of America*. London: Sampson Low, Marston, Searle, & Rivington, 1879.

Churchill, Winston. "Winston Churchill to Lady Randolph Churchill." In Charlotte Gray, *Canada: A Portrait in Letters, 1800-2000*. Toronto: Doubleday Canada, 2003.

Cooley, Dennis. "they leave their traces." In *Bloody Jack*. Edmonton: University of Alberta Press, 2002. First published in Winnipeg by Turnstone Press Ltd., 1984.

Connor, Ralph. *The Foreigner*. Toronto: The Westminster Company Limited, 1909.

Culleton, Beatrice. *In Search of April Raintree*. Winnipeg: Portage & Main Press, 1992. First published by Pemmican Publications, Winnipeg, 1983.

Currie, David. *The Letters of Rusticus*. Montreal: John Dougall & Son, 1880.

Daniells, Roy. "Farewell to Winnipeg." *Mosaic, a Journal for the Interdisciplinary Study of Literature* 3, 3 (Spring 1970): 217.

Durkin, Douglas. *The Magpie*. Toronto: Hodder & Stoughton Limited, 1923.

Fitzgibbon, Mary Agnes. *A Trip to Manitoba*. London: Richard Bentley and Son, 1880.

Fiorentino, Jon Paul. *transcona fragments*. Winnipeg: Cyclops Press, 2002.

Forer, Mort. *The Humback*. Toronto: McClelland & Stewart, 1969.

Francis, Marvin. *city treaty*. Winnipeg: Turnstone Press, 2002.

Friesen, Patrick. "Valour Road." In *St. Mary at Main*. Winnipeg: Muses Company, 1998.

Gray, James H. *Red Lights on the Prairies.* Saskatoon: Fifth House Ltd., 1995. First published in Toronto by MacMillan of Canada, 1971.

Grove, Frederick Philip. *Settlers of the Marsh.* Toronto: The Ryerson Press, 1925.

Gunn, J.J. *Echoes of the Red.* Toronto: The Macmillan Company of Canada, Limited, at St. Martin's House, 1930.

Haas, Maara. "The Green Roses Kerchief." In *Made in Manitoba: An Anthology of Short Fiction.* Winnipeg: Turnstone Press, 1996.

_____. *The Street Where I Live.* Toronto: McGraw-Hill Ryerson Ltd., 1976.

Hale, Katherine. *Canadian Cities of Romance.* Toronto: McClelland & Stewart, 1922.

Healy, W.J. *Women of Red River.* Winnipeg: The Women's Canadian Club, 1923.

Highway, Tomson. *Kiss of the Fur Queen.* Toronto: Doubleday Canada, 1998.

Hunter, Catherine. *The Dead of Midnight.* Winnipeg: Turnstone Press, 2001.

_____. *Lunar Wake.* Winnipeg: Turnstone Press, 1994.

Hunter, Robert. *Erebus.* Toronto: McClelland & Stewart Ltd., 1968.

Ingersoll, William E. *Daisy Herself.* Toronto: The Musson Book Co., Limited, 1920.

Jarvis, W.H.P. *The Letters of a Remittance Man to His Mother.* Toronto: The Musson Book Co., Limited, 1909.

Kleiman, Ed. *The Immortals.* Edmonton: NeWest Press, 1980.

Kroetsch, Robert. "The Winnipeg Zoo." In *Completed Field Notes.* Toronto: McClelland & Stewart Ltd., 1989.

Krotz, Larry. *Shutter Speed.* Winnipeg: Turnstone Press, 1988.

Laurence, Margaret. *Dance on the Earth.* Toronto: McClelland & Stewart Ltd., 1989.

_____. "Main Street Car." *Prairie Fire* 20, 2 (July 1999).

Leacock, Stephen Butler. *My Discovery of the West.* Toronto: Thomas Allen, 1937.

Leah, Vince. *Pages from the Past.* Winnipeg: Winnipeg Tribune, 1975.

Livesay, Dorothy. *A Winnipeg Childhood.* Winnipeg: Peguis Publishers, 1973.

Ludwig, Jack. *Requiem for Bibul.* New York: Dell Publishing Co. Inc. Originally published in *The Atlantic Monthly,* 1960.

Lysenko, Vera. *Yellow Boots.* Edmonton: Canadian Institute of Ukrainian Studies Press/NeWest Press, 1992. First published in Toronto by Ryerson Press, 1954.

MacBeth, R.G. *The Making of the Canadian West: Reminiscences of an Eye-Witness.* Toronto: William Briggs, 1898.

MacLennan, Hugh. *Two Solitudes.* Macmillian Company of Canada Limited, Toronto, 1972.

McDougall, John. *Saddle, Sled and Snowshoe: Pioneering on the Saskatchewan in the Sixties.* Cincinnati: Jennings and Graham, 1896.

Maddin, Guy. "Factoid 1919." *Border Crossings* 77 (2001).

Maynard, Fredelle Bruser. *Raisins and Almonds.* Toronto: Paperjacks, 1973.

_____. "That Sensual Music." In *Winnipeg Stories.* Winnipeg: Queenston House, 1974.

Marlyn, John. *Under the Ribs of Death.* Toronto: McClelland & Stewart Ltd., 1957.

Miller, Henry. *The Tropic of Cancer.* New York: Grove Press, 1934.

Parr, John. *Jim Tweed.* Winnipeg: Queenston House Publishing Co. Ltd., 1978.

Peter, John. *Take Hands at Winter.* New York: Doubleday, 1967.

Reaney, James. "Winnipeg Seen as a Body of Time and Space." In *Selected Shorter Poems.* Erin, ON: Press Porcépic, 1975.

Ross, Alexander. *The Red River Settlement: Its Rise, Progress, and Present State.* Edmonton: Hurtig Publishers, 1972.

Rolyat, Jane. *The Lily of Fort Garry.* London: J.M. Dent and Sons, 1930.

Salverson, Laura Goodman. *The Viking Heart.* Toronto: McClelland & Stewart Inc., 1975.

Samson, John. "One Great City." From *Reconstruction Site.* Toronto: Epitaph Records, 2003.

Sandiland, John. *Western Canadian Dictionary and Phrasebook.* Edmonton: University of Alberta Press, 1977.

Seton, Ernest Thompson. *Animal Heroes.* Toronto: Morang & Company, Limited, 1905.

Shields, Carol. *The Republic of Love.* Toronto: Random House of Canada, 1992.

Sinclair, Gordon. *Cowboys and Indians: The Shooting of J.J. Harper.* Toronto: McClelland & Stewart Ltd., 1999.

Stead, Robert. *The Cowpuncher.* Toronto: The Musson Book Company Limited, 1918.

Sproxton, Birk. *The Red-Headed Woman with the Black, Black Heart.* Winnipeg: Turnstone Press, 1997.

Sweatman, Margaret. *Fox.* Winnipeg: Turnstone Press, 1991.

Tefs, Wayne. *The Canasta Players.* Winnipeg: Turnstone Press, 1990.

Toews, Miriam. *Summer of My Amazing Luck.* Winnipeg: Turnstone Press, 1996.

Young, George. *Manitoba Memories: Leaves from My Life in the Prairie Province, 1868-1884.* Toronto: William Briggs, 1897.

Walsh, Meeka. "Light Reading." *Prairie Fire* 20, 2 (July 1999).

Wiebe, Armin. *The Salvation of Yasch Siemens.* Winnipeg: Turnstone Press, 1984.

Wiebe, Rudy and Yvonne Johnson. *Stolen Life: The Journey of a Cree Woman.* Toronto: Random House of Canada, 1998.

Whittier, John Greenleaf. "The Red River Voyageur." In George Young, *Manitoba Memories: Leaves from My Life in the Prairie Province, 1868-1884.* Toronto: William Briggs, 1897.

Williamson, Dave. *Accountable Advances.* Winnipeg: Turnstone Press, 1994.

Wiseman, Adele. *The Sacrifice.* Toronto: Macmillan of Canada, 1956.

_____. *Crackpot.* Toronto: McClelland & Stewart, 1974.

Waddington, Miriam. *Driving Home: Poems New and Selected.* Toronto: Oxford University Press, 1972.

Credits & Permissions

Turnstone Press would like to acknowledge the following archives, individuals, publications, and companies for the following author photographs and illustrations:

ARCHIVES OF MANITOBA
Beynon, Francis Marion (N13687)
Butler, William Francis (N10493)
Churchill, Winston (Churchill, Winston 2)
Connor, Ralph (N4575)
Hale, Katherine
McDougall, John
Ross, Alexander
Seton, Ernest Thompson (N3664)
Stead, Robert J.C.
Waddington, Miriam (Jewish Historical Society 2958)
Young, George (N657)

UNIVERSITY OF MANITOBA ARCHIVES AND SPECIAL COLLECTIONS
Winnipeg Tribune Collection
Daniels, Roy (18-10106-002)
Forer, Mort (Forer, Mort)
Grove, Frederick Philip
Hunter, Robert (Hunter, Bob)
Laurence, Margaret
Leacock, Stephen Butler
Leah, Vince (Leah, Vince)
Livesay, Dorothy
Ludwig, Jack (Ludwig, Dr. Jack)
Lysenko, Vera (Lysenko, Vera)
MacLennan, Hugh (MacLennan, Hugh)
Peter, John (Peter, Prof J.D.)
Reaney, James (Reaney, James)
Wiseman, Adele

Maynard, Fredelle Bruser (PC 143 #2)
Zolf, Larry (Canadian Press-wire photo, Zolf)

NATIONAL ARCHIVES OF CANADA
Begg, Alexander

WESTERN CANADIAN PICTORIAL INDEX
Ingersoll, William Ernest (A1306-39104)

BORDER CROSSINGS
Walsh, Meeka
Maddin, Guy

SIGNATURE EDITIONS
Amabile, George

COACH HOUSE BOOKS
Jon Paul Fiorentino

WINNIPEG FREE PRESS
Sinclair, Gordon

Arnason, David photo: Angela Browne
Birdsell, Sandra photo: Don Hall
Culleton, Beatrice photo: Deborah E. Culleton
Durkin, Douglas Leader *Canadian Singers and Their Songs* (1919)
Fitzgibbon, Mary Agnes *Types of Canadian Women* (1903)
Friesen, Patrick photo: Marjike Friesen
Gray, James H. photo: courtesy Pat Fennell
Gunn, J.J., *Echoes of the Red* (1930)
Haas, Maara photo: Vienna Badiuk
Highway, Tomson photo: Michael Cooper
Hunter, Catherine photo: Melody Morrissette
McLuhan, Marshall photo: courtesy, Estate of Marshall McLuhan
Salverson, Laura Goodman *Canadian Singers and Their Songs* (1919)
Samson, John photo: Jon Schledewitz
Shields, Carol photo: Neil Graham
Sweatman, Margaret photo: Debra Mosher
Tefs, Wayne photo: Kristin Wittman
Toews, Miriam photo: Andrew Sikorsky

INDEX